DAY OF THE DIESELS
Volume 3: The 1980s

DAY OF THE DIESELS
Volume 3: The 1980s

John Spencer Gilks

Edited by Mike Esau

· RAILWAY HERITAGE ·
from
The NOSTALGIA Collection

First published in 2007

British Library Cataloguing in Publication Data

A catalogue record for this book is available from the British Library.

ISBN 978 1 85794 286 6

Silver Link Publishing Ltd
The Trundle
Ringstead Road
Great Addington
Kettering
Northants NN14 4BW

Tel/Fax: 01536 330588
email: sales@nostalgiacollection.com
Website: www.nostalgiacollection.com

The number appended to each caption is the negative number. Requests for prints may be made via the Publishers.

Printed and bound in Great Britain

Half title Kildale, North Yorks; Class 31 No 31299, 6 April 1983.
The penultimate freight to Whitby accelerates away from the crossing at New Row. This is the second photograph to be taken in retirement, and I cannot believe my good fortune. It's a really sunny day, I'm in my bright red Ford XR3 and have survived an icy down gradient from the Bilsdale road. The train consists of one coal wagon to Sleights, which – even in 1983 – will be pushed into the yard with a pole beneath the wheels! *6847*

Page 2 Garve, Highland; Class 37 No 37261 with eastbound 'Royal Scotsman' meets No 37262 on 10.50 Inverness-Kyle of Lochalsh, 20 May 1985.
This is the first run of the special with its vintage coaches and Trevor Owen and I decided to pursue it from its late start in Edinburgh the previous Wednesday until it passed beneath us near Blair Atholl the following Tuesday. Presumably the postman has brought the mail from Ullapool. *10950*

Title page Selside, North Yorks; Class 40, up empty newspaper vans, 4 December 1983.
The vans are returning from Glasgow over the Settle & Carlisle during a West Coast Main Line diversion weekend. Gavin and I used to enjoy these weekends anticipating the end of the S&C by filming the additional trains at as many locations as possible. We would return home on Sunday with a high tea at The Crown in Helmsley. *8737*

Below left The author by 'Mary' of the 'Yorkshire Pullman' on the Keighley & Worth Valley Railway on 11 June 1988, and near Lugton on the Beith branch on 30 August 1992 – a special DMU will be coming along the rusty track soon, believe it or not! *10010/4*

Below right Acheilidh Crossing, Highland; Classes 26 and 37, 11.15 Wick/11.18 Thurso-Inverness, 31 August 1980.
I'm en route from the Invershin Hotel to Gullane and drop off at Aviemore to buy a carpet, which graced the guest bedroom for years. *11141*

CONTENTS

Pyewipe Junction, Lincoln; DMU, 10.26 Doncaster-Sleaford, 10 October 1984.
I have walked along the track from Holmes Crossing, and a platelayer commented that he had never seen a track permit, so could he see mine! I was able to oblige. The vandals have been here first. The distant signal and the S-bend in the permanent way are all that remind us of the former junction here of the Lancashire, Derbyshire & East Coast route from, say, Chesterfield, and the Lincoln avoiding line. Today there is a spur from here towards Newark for use when the East Coast Main Line is subject to major engineering works and diversions are necessary. *6149*

Holgate Road bridge, York; Class 31 No 31118, ballast train, 26 May 1988.
This was a popular vantage point for young trainspotters who brought their sandwiches and spent a harmless day here. Now the area is encased in high metal fencing. A sign of the times perhaps, but electrification is a danger. *4539*

INTRODUCTION

As this is the seventh book in the 'Dawn of the Diesels' and 'Day of the Diesels' series I do not propose to repeat the basis on which it is written but would refer new readers to earlier editions – in much the same way as students participating in *University Challenge* are adjudged to be aware of the rules!

In looking at the following illustrations of railway operations I would like to comment on a number of issues that I consider significant in this regard during 2006.

First is the decision of Eddie Stobart Ltd, the great road haulier, to launch a dedicated rail freight service contracted to Tesco plc between Daventry and Grangemouth every weekday for three years, commencing on 19 September 2006. I photographed this at the site of Hincaster Junction on 20 October and it looked fine, every wagon bearing the legend 'less CO_2'. According to the press handout one trainload is equivalent to 28 trucks in volume, which would have travelled 19,600 miles. It has always seemed to me that when the motorways are gridlocked –which some are already at certain times of day – the number of private motorists who vote will outweigh the lorry drivers and owners, so they are on the losing side. However, if road pricing is introduced road hauliers will be able to pass on the costs in a way that most individual motorists will be unable to do. The shortage of HGV drivers and the working time directive has swung the balance back towards rail, and road/rail depots are being built in various parts of the UK.

In the light of this situation I tried to contact the British Road Federation, the powerful lobby on behalf of road interests, only to be informed by the BT Enquiry Line that they had ceased to exist! A call to the Chartered Institute of Logistics & Transport (UK) – of which I am a Fellow – discovered that the BRF had so lost members that it had become a segment of the CBI (Confederation of British Industry). Its staff had formed the Road Users Alliance Ltd, whose principal object is 'to promote, support and actively encourage the implementation of a national strategy for personal and commercial mobility in the UK which recognises the need for substantial enhancement of road, foot and cycle path capacity in an integrated travel system.' I have yet to discover which groups form the alliance and how the integrated system incorporates railways.

The third item of special interest was a BBC Radio 4 programme on 3 September 2006. Entitled *Reunion*, it brought together five of the principal participants in the privatisation of BR. In the course of the discussion Sue MacGregor asked John Welsby, last Chairman & Chief Executive of BR as a national concern, 'How much were you, with all your British Rail experience and expertise, consulted about all this?' The answer was, 'Not at all; not – at – all.' When the former Minister took exception to this, Welsby elaborated by saying, 'We had one meeting, in a hotel in Petty France, one afternoon.' Nicholas Ridley, a former Transport Minister, had said of BR that 'they're not an industry, they're a service'. In my opinion it is not unfair to say that 150 years of knowledge and acquired experience of railways was trashed in six weeks. Welsby said he did not know who had contrived the privatisation proposals. At the time Jeremy Paxman interviewed a Mr Ken Irvine on *Newsnight*. When asked whether he was responsible, he shifted on his chair and, when pressed, agreed that it was he. Who and where he is, I know not.

And finally there is the question of the UK all-line railway timetable. Network Rail has announced that the last of these will appear in the Summer of 2007. Has there ever been another company that has positively decided not to advertise its wares? Will the individual franchisees publish their own timetables as in the days before BR? Access to the internet is not the same, and according to Andrew Dow in the Autumn 2006 *Journal of the Friends of the National Railway Museum*, the staff at Transport Direct assume ignorance on the part of the traveller. Bradshaw ceased years ago, and the ABC – now the only survivor is to go. It heralds a further break-up of the integrated rail system we have taken for granted.

In conclusion, can I thank Peter Townsend, Will Adams and Mick Sanders for their part in producing this book, and my editor Mike Esau, who never tires of helping me. Then there is John Edgington and Trevor Owen. And this time a special thank you to the National Railway Museum – and especially Andrew Scott and Simon Batchelor – for allowing me to research timetables during their difficult time while the Search Engine project is pursued. The logo is designed by Gavin Mist.

John Gilks
Nawton, 2007

Canterbury East, Kent.
Note the destination indicator for the 09.04 to Liverpool (Lime Street) (see page 10).

1.
SOUTH AND WEST

I have a good friend in London – Dr Ian Cantlon. Now that I live in North Yorkshire he is kind enough to seek out any location I require in the south and take appropriate pictures. He is very painstaking and I am fortunate to receive his results. In the spring of 1997 he made three visits to Waterloo to secure views of the Penzance sleeper when it terminated there for a short time to connect with trains to Europe. This meant an early start from his home, and he doesn't drive – he even went on to Vauxhall to record the passing of the empty stock to Old Oak Common! Then in 2005 he took himself at least once to Wandsworth Road and Farningham Road stations to photograph the Channel Tunnel trains while they still ran that way prior to transfer in 2007 to St Pancras, and the abandonment of Waterloo International. Presumably continental freight will use the Fawkham Junction spur line. Now I have asked him to go to Greenford to picture the train that only runs five times a week along the single line from Old Oak Common to the junction at South Ruislip. Greenford is served by a shuttle from Ealing Broadway via Castle Bar Park, and by the Central Line. So far, due to the encroachment of the environment, he has been unable to obtain a shot, but in due course I am sure he will succeed.

Another photographer perfectionist is Graham Vincent of Bath. He kindly went to the single line between Thingley Junction and Trowbridge via Melksham to record West of England traffic (and trains from the Somerset quarries) during a diversion following a level crossing accident in 2004.

I like panoramic views and my favourite in the following selection is from the tower block near Reading station. When I ran an evening class there we visited what at the time was the state-of-the-art signal box.

One of the most significant trains in the following selection in my view is the parcels from Penzance, seen in the St Austell/Lostwithiel area. This contains empty newspaper vans returning to London. With the loss of this traffic and some of that of the Post Office, the co-ordinated transport system bequeathed us by the Victorians is being destroyed bit by bit.

Returning to connections at Waterloo with Channel Tunnel traffic, I recall using the short-lived 10.46 train, bound for Cardiff, to reach Reading. It was an HST. I boarded and took my seat in a totally empty Coach E as an announcement was made that the buffet was now open for the sale of this and that. I fancied a hot chocolate, so made my way to the next coach. The attendant was obviously surprised to see me, but pleased that his announcement had not fallen on deaf ears. When we were under way and the ticket collector appeared I enquired how many passengers were on board. 'Five,' he said, 'and you are the only one to have paid. The others are railway staff!'

Incidentally, the Penzance sleeper soon reverted to Paddington. In 2006 it was threatened with withdrawal but survived, though the Exeter coach has disappeared. It may be that the regular use of the sleeper by a retired Governor of the Bank of England was relevant.

Above Canterbury East, Kent; Class 47, 09.04 to Liverpool (Lime Street), 5 October 1987.

This train ran as empty coaching stock (ECS) from Willesden and took passengers from here. I was the only one that day, and in the 1st Class coach. When I ventured to the buffet after leaving Dover I found the attendant on the verge of tears. It was a Monday and during the weekend vandals had entered the kitchen and sprayed everywhere with tomato ketchup. It was a terrible mess and he had spent the journey from London trying to clear up, but still could not serve. He had rung his depot to bring more provisions to the train at Olympia, and when I alighted there he was duly met. The train had travelled via Tonbridge and the Darent Valley to Bromley South. I have reason to believe that the handful of London bypass trains at this time were an indulgence of the then Chief Executive of BR, though they had to make money. Sadly they were soon withdrawn and I was glad of my photographs here and there in the south. *325/5*

Below Hildenborough, Kent; Class 47 No 47519, 07.40 Manchester (Piccadilly)-Dover (Western Docks), 9 February 1988.

This is another of the trains mentioned above, and didn't operate for long. The woods surrounding the station had been devastated by the infamous gale. *363/2*

Above Oxted, Surrey; DEMU No 205001, 16.38 Uckfield-London Bridge, 15 October 1986.

As mentioned in *Day of the Diesels* Volume 2, page 9, weekday trains on the Uckfield line now provide a through service to London, whereas at the time of the picture these only operated at peak hours – real progress. 80

Below Lingfield, Surrey; DEMU No 207009, 13.36 Victoria-East Grinstead, 15 October 1986.

Electrification has replaced the diesel units here, and I suspect the semaphore signals may have been superseded too. Gone are the days when special steam trains came to the races, some with Pullman cars for lunch and marshalled at the head of the up train so that the bookmakers could make a quick getaway! 88

Left **East Grinstead, West Sussex; DEMU No 204002, 16.17 to London Bridge, 15 October 1986.**
The trains have terminated here since the strike of 1955 except for the period when Miss Bessemer forced the Southern Region to eat humble pie and provide a service of four return trips to Lewes. Hitherto trains also ran regularly to Haywards Heath via Horsted Keynes from time to time. But soon the Bluebell Railway will reach here and we shall be able again to travel through to Sheffield Park. 98

Below **Rye, East Sussex; DEMU No 1319, 12.49 Hastings-Ashford, 12 January 1980.**
Sadly it is typical of government attitudes to railways that the 25 miles of this line have not been electrified and that the A259 trunk road has not been diverted at East Guldeford to eliminate two level crossings.

When the Channel Tunnel opened and Ashford International station came into being, the trains were extended to Brighton to facilitate travel to Europe. Then they were cut back, first to Eastbourne and later to Hastings. Today they run through to and from Brighton again. Perhaps it turns on the availability of diesel units. 388

Above Tunbridge Wells West, Kent; DEMU No 1317,
10.59 Eridge-Tonbridge, 7 June 1985.

The station buildings were still lit by gas on my visit and towered above
their surroundings as the London, Brighton & South Coast Railway
boasted its superiority over the South Eastern through the tunnel down
the road (but which has survived!). A supermarket now stands
adjacent. When the Council discussed the planning application for
this I suggested that perhaps the single line to Grove Junction could be
encased in the new building, but I could see that they had already made
up their minds to consent without such a condition. A preservation
service has come into being westwards. *124*

Below Birchden Junction, East Sussex; DEMU No 1317,
12.59 Eridge-Tonbridge, 7 June 1985.

It would have been as photographer to the Friends of the National
Railway Museum that I made my way with a track permit to this spot.
The junction was with the main line from Oxted to the coast.
Strangely enough the tracks north of here were used to store
locomotives for years, and the through service from London did not
exist. *129*

Above Overton, Hants; Class 50, 15.13 Salisbury-Waterloo,
8 September 1989.

When Stanley Raymond (later Chairman BRB) was put in charge of the Western Region he was determined that Paddington should be the exclusive gateway to the West of England, and because his boundary crossed the Southern west of Salisbury he was able to engineer the destruction of the excellent service from Waterloo. He even had the 'Atlantic Coast Express' terminated at Salisbury. But local people have fought back – though see page 103 of *I Tried to Run a Railway* by G. F. Fiennes (Ian Allan, 1967) – and a modernised service now connects Waterloo with Exeter. *1015B*

Left Whitchurch, Hants; Class 50
No 50026 *Indomitable*, 14.22 Exeter
St David's-Waterloo, 8 September 1989.
This station used to be called Whitchurch North, to distinguish it from its counterpart on the Didcot, Newbury & Southampton line (closed in 1960). It was also the terminating point for Longparish and Fullerton Junction (on the Andover/Romsey line) until 1931 – note the island platform on the up side. *1019A*

Above Exeter Central, Devon; DMU, 12.35 to Exmouth,
13 September 1980.
The branch to Exmouth is the one line that I have never travelled
(outside some conurbations) in mainland UK. At one time (until
1967) it was possible to travel a 'horseshoe' and regain the main line at
Sidmouth Junction. As its name implies, this station is much better
sited for the city centre than St David's. *1162*

Below Exeter Central, Devon; Class 50, 09.00 Waterloo-Exeter
St David's, 13 September 1980.
I'm attending a conference organised by the Royal Town Planning
Institute at the University and have come out of a session for a break.
For some years I gave a slide show professionally as an evening session
and well recall two events. One was an approach from the Divisional
Manager, Reading, who asked me where and when I had taken a view
near Sonning with a tree branch overhanging the track to a potentially
dangerous degree; the other was a delegate at a later session who
condemned his colleagues for allowing the environment to become so
ugly between London and Slough! *1160*

Above **Newton St Cyres, Devon; Class 25, 12.38 Barnstaple-Exeter Central, 13 September 1980.**
I have already mentioned Stanley Raymond and the Western Region, and it was he who achieved closure of the network in West Devon, including the alternative route from Exeter to Plymouth. To argue that this duplicated the route along the coast just ignored the significance of Okehampton, Tavistock and their hinterland. What a legacy! Even John Betjeman was denied his beloved journey to Padstow. *1166*

Left **Easton Barton, Devon; Class 31, 14.45 Barnstaple-Paddington, 13 September 1980.**
When the direct service was withdrawn between Taunton and Barnstaple in 1966, it was thought that the through train from London to Ilfracombe would disappear. Hitherto the service had operated from Waterloo, but instead it ran from Paddington with reversal at Exeter. Imagine the surprise, therefore, when it continued to run after the closure too of Ilfracombe (1970), but here it is with its homeward-bound holidaymakers. It's Saturday afternoon, so the conference in Exeter is adjourned. *1169*

Right **High Wycombe, Bucks; DMU, diverted 14.10 Marylebone-Aylesbury, 26 June 1982.**

I have always been impressed by the height and quality of the retaining wall on the east of the railway here, which I suspect dates from the development of part of the Maidenhead-Oxford branch to become the GWR main line from Paddington to Birmingham (partly jointly with the Great Central Railway) in 1906. The lines avoiding the platforms have since been lifted. When I chartered a special train from Kingston to Kidderminster through the Southern, Western and London Midland Regions, it failed to stop at West Ruislip and I had to ask the driver to back into the platform to pick up one of my guests. It then occurred to me that his working timetable omitted not only this call but a later one at High Wycombe. This was more serious as we might avoid the platform, so he was good enough to phone ahead and David Short duly joined the DMU. *2317*

Below **Reading, Berks; HST, 14.45 Weston-super-Mare-Paddington, 14 July 1980.**

The fine old signal box guards the junction for Basingstoke and Westbury (and the carriage sidings). It is a Monday afternoon and, prior to entertaining the Manager of Reading Transport to dinner, I've come up into the tower –then part BR – at the peak hour. What a view! (See also page I of the colour section.) Reading must be one of the busiest stations in the South East, and there was a time when every bay platform housed a train most hours. Since 1965 the Southern services from Waterloo and Redhill (Gatwick) have been transferred from Reading (Southern); originally these shared just one platform so that the Redhill service had to come and go during the electric train layover. *1620*

Left Bradford-on-Avon, Wilts; Class 33, 16.30 Westbury-Cardiff General, 25 July 1981.
Before the construction of the direct Great Western line to the west at the turn of the 20th century, Westbury was the point at which the Wilts, Somerset & Weymouth Railway shed its branch to Salisbury, which, soon after nationalisation, was transferred to the Southern Region. The station buildings here owe their origin to Brunel himself and date from 1874 with broad gauge track. Note the tunnel from which trains emerge straight on to a road crossing at the eastern portal. *2157*

Below Sea Mills, Avon; DMU, single-car DMU, 11.35 Bristol (Temple Meads)-Severn Beach, 3 April 1982.
This photograph was taken on the spring outing by coach of the 'Talking of Trains' class at Surbiton, and you can trace our route through the photographs of this book, ending with fish and chips at Thame in Oxfordshire. This is a joint line of the Great Western & Midland, and until 1965 there was an eastbound extension to Kingswood Junction on the then main line to Mangotsfield, Bath and the north (now lifted). In the other direction the Great Western continued from Avonmouth to Hallen Marsh and (until 1968) to Pilning on the tracks to the Severn Tunnel. Today the service is still unusual, being throughout on Saturdays but midweek, outside the peak, a bus connection is provided between Avonmouth and Severn Beach. *2177*

Above Patchway, Avon; HST, 11.41 Swansea-Paddington,
3 April 1982.
The coach has moved on a little and we are now above the west end of
Patchway Tunnels. Do notice that the up line is graded separately to
assist the climb from the Severn Tunnel. When I chartered a DMU
over the Central Wales line, a passenger joined and alighted at
Patchway, it being the only common station on the outward run via
Hereford and the return journey via Westbury. *2966*

Below Awre, Glos; Class 47, westbound ballast engineers train,
13 June 1988.
I've trespassed on to the steps of the signal box (unmanned) to take
this picture around lunchtime. The train has come from Gloucester
and is heading towards Chepstow. I'm staying at the Radnorshire Arms
in Presteigne, where the oak in the bar is so ancient that it is as hard as
iron. Later I went on to Llangollen and Matlock. *2272*

Above Tyntesfield, Avon; Class 47, 08.20 Plymouth-Leeds, 25 July 1981.
This name has become famous for the recent National Trust acquisition of an estate of which the mansion has remained untouched for years, though inhabited, so that it represents an era long past. I've stayed overnight at the Swan Hotel in Wells, having come there from a professional engagement in Henley the previous day. My diary does not describe the event, but does say 'free by 3pm'! I went home to Kingston via Bradford-on-Avon (see above, page 18) 2186

Left Worle Junction, Avon; Class 47, 11.35 Paignton-Manchester (Piccadilly), 25 July 1981.
I've driven west and this train is emerging from the loop through Weston-super-Mare. It is a Summer Saturday so there are some additional holiday trains. 2199

Above Bleadon & Uphill, Avon; Class 47, 07.55 Penzance-Liverpool (Lime Street), 25 July 1981.

This lofty bridge, which springs from the cutting, is a famous landmark on Brunel's Bristol & Exeter Line of 1841. The station closed in October 1964. Beyond here the line curves south along more level ground near the sea. *2204*

Below Newbury Race Course, Berks; HST, 11.25 Paddington-Penzance 'Cornish Riviera Express', January 1980.

This station has happy memories for me. I had written an article in *The Railway Enthusiast*, the magazine of the club in Farnborough, Hants, describing the link between railway promoters and racing in the Southern Region, which prompted a letter from Cyril Rider, PRO of the Western, proclaiming their interest too. He invited me to travel on a racegoers' special – 1st Class – from Paddington on 13 August 1954 to meet an Inspector who would explain the special workings (from the South Wales coalfield and Oxford, for example). Little did I realise that this was to begin a long association with BR management. *1659*

Above Kintbury, Berks; Class 50, 12.25 Paddington-Plymouth, January 1980.
There is little to say about this picture except that the weather is dull and the Kennet & Avon Canal looks full of boats. *1679*

Below Exeter St David's, Devon; Class 45 No 45008, 10.35 Paignton-Leeds/Hull, 13 September 1980.
This is the Saturday when the planning conference had an afternoon free, and I seem to have spent most of the day by the railway. The level crossing on which I am standing spreads across many tracks and is so often closed that cars tend to find other ways over the line. In the evening we all visited the Maritime Museum. *1820*

Above Forder Viaduct, Cornwall; Class 47 No 47501,
06.45 Swindon-Penzance, 21 April 1988.
Trevor Owen and I have rented Whiteford Temple, a Landmark Trust
property near Callington, which is well sited north of the main line
and with ease of access both east and west. Today we explore the
Saltash peninsula, Lostwithiel and, inevitably, Golant on the Fowey
branch, before the bungalow was built in the strategic field! *1882*

Below Liskeard, Cornwall; Class 47 No 47553, up engineer's
train, 17 April 1988.
Standing on the down main, the train is about to complete its Sunday
work and head for Plymouth. The line falls steeply west on leaving the
platform end. In the morning we travelled on the Launceston Steam
Railway. *1924*

Above Tarras Crossing, Cornwall; single-car DMU, 18.47 Liskeard-Looe, 22 April 1988.

It's our last day in Callington. The branch line to Looe was recommended for closure in the first Beeching Report of 1963 (page 106), but it has proved impossible to implement owing to the nature of the terrain and the narrow roads that any substitute bus would have to negotiate. Not that it isn't always under review. The musical instrument museum at St Keyne has helped the tourist traffic. *1912*

Below Moorswater Viaduct, Cornwall; HST, 15.50 Paddington-Penzance, 19 April 1988.

Trains from Liskeard to Looe reverse at Coombe, where there is a junction with the line from the quarries that passes beneath this viaduct. According to the previous 'Freightmaster', loaded cement tanks arrive each week from Earles Sidings (in the Hope Valley between Sheffield and Manchester) in the early hours of a Thursday and return empty from here at 15.30 the same day. *1927*

B3269, south of Milltown, Cornwall; DMU, 16.58 Plymouth-Penzance, 21 April 1988.
The train is heading into Treverran Tunnel, while the viaduct in the background spans a stream that is about to enter the River Fowey. If you walk beneath its arches you come upon the Lostwithiel-Fowey branch within a few yards at ground level by the water. The china clay trains pass beneath us here, reverse in Lostwithiel, then go south (or vice versa). 1961

Above Restormel, Cornwall; Class 50 No 50015 *Valiant*, up vans, 21 April 1988.
As we will see later in St Austell, this train conveys empty newspaper vans back to London in the early afternoon. Because the last picture takes a full page we have gone backwards in our geographical sequence! *1939*

Left Par, Cornwall; HST, 13.44 Penzance-Paddington, and single-car DMU, 14.47 to Newquay, 19 April 1988.
On one occasion I joined this train to Newbury, then doubled back to Kintbury for the night. Snoozing in a nearby seat was John Amis, one-time Secretary to the conductor Sir Thomas Beecham and participant in the BBC TV series *My Music*. Last year I reminded him of this meeting. 'What did I reply to your "hello"?' 'You grunted!' The branch from here to Newquay still has through HSTs at holiday times, but otherwise a single car at infrequent intervals suffices. *1969*

Above B3374, Mount Charles, Cornwall; Class 50 No 50035 *Ark Royal*, up vans, 19 April 1988.
I like this train, which we saw first in St Austell station, then again here, and two days later near Restormel. *1985*

Below St Austell, Cornwall; Class 50, up local, 19 April 1988.
The yard used to provide stabling for Motorail trains, which terminated here from London and the North. Why have we discontinued these? Motorway driving has no pleasure. *1987*

Above Burngullow, Cornwall; Class 37 No 37414 shunting china clay tanks, 24 October 1989.

I've come here at the invitation of BR to take photographs for its freight magazine. The yard master – 'Gonzo' – asked me to lunch with him at Par, but could not drive me there at the time, so arranged with the driver of this '37 to take me in his cab with the tanks. I was impressed by the weight of the train as we pulled away. But there was a problem! My suitcases were in the left luggage office at St Austell and had to be collected if I was to go on from Par to Newbury. No problem! The Class 37 halted at the foot of the staircase (inevitably the office was on the far platform), I sprinted over the footbridge and back again duly laden, and we headed for Par. *1997B*

Left Burngullow Junction, Cornwall; Class 50 No 50021 *Rodney*, up vans (yet again!), 18 April 1988.

At this point the permanent way was narrowed from two to a single track as far as Probus in the interests of economy. The second track has now been restored and one wonders how much this cost. The right-hand line went to Drinnick Mill. *2000*

Above Coombe St Stephen Viaduct, Cornwall; Class 50
No 50023 *Howe*, Penzance-Bristol parcels, 22 April 1988.
You can still see the supports of the original timber viaduct on the left
of the later structure. Not much traffic for the Midlands today. *2010*

Below Grampound Road station site, Cornwall; HST,
13.44 Penzance-Paddington, 22 April 1988.
This station was totally closed from 5 October 1964. The village is
about 5 miles away on the A390 and a new community had been built
up by the railway. *2013*

Above Truro, Cornwall; Class 50 No 50019 *Ramillies*, 18.30 Penzance-Birmingham, 20 April 1988.
This was to be our last picture of the day before returning along the A30 back to Callington, and we were lucky that the sun continued to shine until quite late. 2019

Below Carnon Viaduct, Cornwall; DMU, 18.07 Truro-Falmouth, 20 April 1988.
Again it is possible to see the supports of the earlier viaduct in the foreground. What a superb structure, one of a number to enhance the local environment. 2023

Right Hayle, Cornwall; DMU,
12.42 Plymouth-Penzance, 20 April 1988.
The sea is just down to the left of the picture
and the River Hayle flows from under the
bridge. Nice to see a Metro-Cammell unit
finishing its days in the country. *2035*

Below Penzance, Cornwall; Class 47, **10.27 Penzance-Edinburgh
and Glasgow, 20 April 1988.**
We can go no further than here. Do notice the Travelling Post Office
coaches in the siding. In the quest to rid passenger trains of locomotive
haulage, the London sleeper was recently threatened with withdrawal.
It is safe for now, but the sleeping cars attached at Plymouth and at
Exeter are no more. *2062*

2.
WALES

I have always thought that the Beeching closure of the lines between Carmarthen and Aberystwyth and between Afon Wen and Menai Bridge led to the growth in Welsh nationalism, which resulted in devolution to Cardiff in recent years. Great emphasis is now laid on the through service connecting Cardiff (07.20) with Holyhead (12.20), and Holyhead (14.35) with Cardiff (19.28) on weekdays. There is also one train each way on Sundays. There is no alternative than to run it from north of Abergavenny to just west of Chester through England.

The area west of Carmarthen has always fascinated me and I never fail to visit each year. Generally I relate this to the date of the Royal Agricultural Show at Builth Wells, which results in an extra – proper – train from Cardiff to Llandrindod Wells. When this runs – in July – the daytime Fishguard boat train has usually become of interest too, with its route from Cardiff over the Swansea Avoiding Line to Llanelly. In 2006 both trains were hauled by preserved Class 50 locomotives, at least one of which was leased from the Severn Valley Railway. It shows the high condition of some of the preserved railways. A number of illustrations of the area in the 1980s are reproduced below.

One of the most unusual trains included here must be the empty stock of sleeping cars run from Llandudno Junction to Llandudno in the afternoon to catch up with the InterCity Land Cruise to London. I nearly missed this due to road traffic, but the signalman at Deganwy saw my predicament and delayed clearing the signal for its approach until I had climbed on to the footbridge at the station there! I had travelled on the train a year or two before, so knew the procedure it was likely to follow. In 2006 the Euston/Holyhead/Euston trains were formed of 'Pendolinos', but of course these lacked the availability of overhead electric traction west of Crewe, so were hauled from there by a Class 57. A similar situation existed when these units were diverted from the West Coast Main Line over the Settle & Carlisle route. If this series of books goes on long enough, pictures of these trains will appear in due course! There was also a locomotive-hauled train each day from Manchester to Holyhead and return.

One Welsh picture that has eluded me so far is the 15.02 (TThO) Penyffordd-Healey Mills empty box wagons, where the engine runs round the train in the Croes Newydd loop just south-east of Wrexham General station. This, and other trains, have failed to materialise at the booked time. It is not possible legitimately to park near the site, which is conveniently located under a bridge, and road traffic is deafening while one waits in vain. I will have another go next year!

Above right Nantyhegog, Dyfed; Class 37 No 37312, 09.58 Carmarthen-Milford Haven, 18 April 1981.
I'm staying at a favourite hotel – Plas Glansevin near Llangadog (now converted to an old people's home!) – which I use as a base for visiting the area formerly known as Pembrokeshire. Once west of Carmarthen the atmosphere changes for the better and I'm intrigued by the nature of the lonely countryside away from the coast. This set of coaches was used for a period before sufficient DMUs were available to operate the timetable. *3135*

Right Clarbeston Road, Dyfed; DMU, 11.02 Swansea-Milford Haven, 10 May 1988.
Although the railway to Milford Haven opened in 1854, this place did not become a junction until 1906, when the direct line to Letterston Junction and Fishguard was opened at a time when the Great Western's drive to carry the Irish traffic began in earnest (the Badminton line was also involved). Hitherto trains had diverged north near Clynderwen and wandered through the hills via Maenclochog, a line that became disused in 1949 except at the extreme western end. I changed here in 1961 and took the push-and-pull unit with No 9760 to call at all the halts en route to Fishguard; three years later they were closed and the local service withdrawn. *3188*

Above Spittal Tunnel; DMU, 13.20 Fishguard-Swansea, 12 May 1988.

This tunnel gives access to the valley of the Western Cleddau, which the track threads into the undulating country to the coast. Usually there are only two trains each way per day – one at midday and the other in the early hours – to make boat connections with Rosslare, but at this date there were two at lunchtime for some reason. *3210*

Below Letterston Junction, Dyfed; 'Sprinter' DMU, 14.32 Fishguard-Swansea, 12 May 1988.

A newer unit is seen this time, as the service had originated in Cardiff. The daytime train to Fishguard has varied over the years. In recent times it has been headed by a Class 37, and from Cardiff has taken the Swansea Avoiding Line to Llanelly; in 2005 the stop at Bridgend was omitted. In 2006 a Class 50 was borrowed from the Severn Valley Railway at the height of the season. Once again, if these series of books go on long enough you might see the 2006 views of this train in due course! This is the occasion when the signal box is being demolished; I arrived (with the farmer's consent) just in time. *3227*

Above Pantyffynnon, West Glamorgan; Class 37 shunting branch to Gwaun Cae Gurwen (closed to passengers in 1926), and No 08756 in siding, 14 May 1988.
The signal box here controls all the electrical signalling on the Central Wales Line to Craven Arms. *3245*

Below Pantyffynnon, West Glamorgan; DMU, 10.42 Shrewsbury-Swansea, 14 May 1988.
And here is a train that has experienced all that signalling. On this occasion I have been staying at Tower Hill Lodge – another Landmark Trust property – near Llanarthney. *3250*

Above Llandeilo, Dyfed; DMU, 15.22 Swansea-Shrewsbury, 14 May 1988.
At the back of the town on the south side is a road that runs along a bluff and gives this excellent view of the line in the Afon Tywi valley. There is still a loop here on the single track. *3266*

Below Llandrindod Wells, Powys; DMU, 12.51 Shrewsbury-Swansea, 14 May 1988.
This train was unusual in making its first stop at Knighton, then only at Builth Rd (request), Llanwrtyd, Llandovery, Llandeilo, Ammanford and Pantyffynnon. *3305*

Above **Cynhordy Viaduct, Powys; DMU, 12.51 Shrewsbury-Swansea, 7 May 1988.**
David Lawrence and Gavin Johns are sitting in the front of this train and expect me to pick them up later in Llandeilo. It is an unusual unit for this route and does not appear to be carrying the regulation floodlight. We are heading for Tower Hill Lodge and dinner at Ty Mawr, Brechfa, which was in the *Good Food Guide* that year. *3279*

Below **Cynhordy Viaduct, Powys; DMU, 11.50 Swansea-Shrewsbury, 9 May 1988.**
The unusual unit is returning and I've moved north of the viaduct. In 2006 I saw the annual train to the Royal Agricultural Show at Builth (Road) with its Severn Valley Railway Class 50 near here, and on returning to my car met and had coffee with the Secretary of the Heart of Wales Line Travellers' Association. She told me that the train was 45 minutes late due to overcrowding – passengers were wedged in the Mk 2 coaches and took time to board at the end doors. *3281*

Above Knucklas (Mayope), Powys; DMU, 12.51 Shrewsbury-Swansea, 6 May 1988.

I'm staying in Knucklas and have almost completed a really marvellous walk in the spring sunshine (from 10am until 5pm!). On the way out I met a van on a farm track and cadged a lift up the hill towards Llangunllo. The driver told me that he had given up a job in the City to transport bags of lime round the farms and was very happy now. That morning he had visited four locations where the farmhouses were left unlocked, and in one case there was a purse on the kitchen table. Quite safe! *3332*

Left Bucknell, Salop; DMU, 11.50 Swansea-Shrewsbury, 14 May 1988.

Strictly speaking this picture should not be here as we have crossed the Welsh border, but it completes the Central Wales views so I hope is acceptable! On my first journey on the line – in 1956 – my steam train from Llandovery stopped here and the crew got out to sit in the sun on the station seats. I was the only passenger and asked what was to do. 'Oh,' they replied, 'we take the goods back from here so we have to wait for it to come.' It wasn't long – why didn't I photograph it? *3356*

Right Talerddig, Powys; 'Sprinter' DMU, 09.40 Pwllheli-Birmingham (New Street), 15 June 1988.
We've moved to the former Cambrian line now, and Dennis Lloyd (of Carno) has kindly agreed that I might record him handing the single-line staff to the driver; a procedure soon to be overtaken by electronics. Carno station is the base of the Laura Ashley clothes empire. This is the summit of the line and bankers were usually employed from Machynlleth as far as here on peak Summer Saturdays on steam-hauled holiday trains, and sometimes westbound from Newtown too. *3466*

Below Barmouth, Gwynedd; 'Sprinter' DMU, 16.20 Machynlleth-Pwllheli, 9 August 1987.
This is rather a special day for me. David Lawrence has hired an ex-Great Western saloon and had it coupled to 'The Cardigan Coast Express' excursion from Machynlleth to Pwllheli behind No.7819 *Hinton Manor* – tender-first on return. I agreed to take one end of the saloon for my friends on condition the coach was run round the train at Pwllheli. This was done after some negotiation, which meant that a level crossing was closed to the road for some time. On the outward journey David's guests saw the view through rain, but on the return we were bathed in sunshine all along the coast with nearly an hour at Barmouth when we crossed this DMU. *3552*

Above Valley, Gwynedd; Class 47, up Freightliner, 18 April 1989.
The Landmark Trust property used this time is at Rhiwddolian Ty
Capel and is a disused chapel west of Betws-y-Coed reached by an
unmade road through forestry property – luggage had to be
manhandled over a ladder-stile to reach base. But it was quiet! I was
funded by BR in connection with its freight journal and the purpose
was to picture the branch to Amlwch. You may observe on the right of
this picture new ballast to form a triangle for turning steam engines at
the point where the nuclear flask is handled for road transfer to Wylfa.
3608/15

Above right Holyhead, Gwynedd; Class 47 No 47517,
17.45 Holyhead-Crewe, 18 April 1989.
I'm told that the engine shed has been swept away and that a trunk
road now runs through here to the quayside. These days Virgin
'Pendolinos' operate this service, with a Class 57 on the front at this
point. *3608/24*

Right Rosgoch, Gwynedd; Class 47 No 47227, empty wagons
from Amlwch to Cheshire, 18 April 1989.
We have had a bit of luck. When the daily train joined the main line
at Gaerwen the signalman called out to the effect that the engine
would return later to Amlwch to bring out some empty wagons that
had contained yellow sulphur. And here they are near the derelict
Shell siding. The entire branch is out of use now. *3604/4*

Above Bangor, Gwynedd; Class 47, 10.22 Holyhead-Euston, 10 October 1981.

The station between the tunnels is seen from the well-known viewpoint at the east end. When Harry joined Alan and myself to travel on the goods to Bethesda in 1962 he came from London on the sleeper to Holyhead and returned here in the diner for breakfast. *3615*

Left Llandegi Tunnel, Gwynedd; Class 47, 09.30 Crewe-Holyhead, 10 October 1981.

Having come east through a tunnel into Bangor station, then leaving through another (ending with the junction for Bethesda), the train then enters yet another within a few hundred yards – an expensive piece of line to construct. *3620*

Above right Capel Ogwen road, Gwynedd; Class 40, 11.12 Bangor-Manchester (Victoria), 10 October 1981.

It's a Saturday between conferences. Yesterday I left one in Sheffield, picked up Gavin at Crewe off the 16.50 ex-Euston and began my stay in Llandudno (returning him to London on the 16.46 at Llandudno Junction on the Sunday – it was late and, in the absence of coach J, there was no reserved seat!). Never mind – this was a pleasant sunny day. *3621*

Right Penmaenbach, Gwynedd; 'Sprinter' DMU, 09.04 Greenfield-Bangor, 18 April 1989.

Until I researched the timetable for this train I had not realised that it originated at a wayside station in the Pennines. This occurred because previously it had been a commuter train in Manchester and there was no point running it any further east. *3623/21*

Above Llandudno Junction, Gwynedd; DMU, 11.55 Llandudno-Holyhead, 10 October 1981.

This train is going to reverse direction at the junction. Notice how the line hugs the Conwy estuary. *3641*

Below Deganwy, Gwynedd; Class 47 No 47827, 15.40 ECS sleepers Llandudno Junction-Llandudno, 7 September 1989.

We are in the midst of one of David Ward's Welsh Land Cruises, and very good they were, forming part of the InterCity Special Trains set-up of BR. On Tuesday 5 September departure had been from St Pancras at 19.15 using the Wigston curve and Nuneaton avoiding line during dinner to bring the train ultimately to Shrewsbury station for the night. Here the sleepers stood in the little-used platform adjacent to the main building. Next day the train made the circuit of the Central Wales Line, Hereford and Crewe to stable at Llandudno Junction overnight. When the train sallied forth ECS to Blaenau Ffestiniog, the sleepers were left behind, so in the afternoon had to be re-united with the main train in the terminus at Llandudno. Here they are making that move. It was only with assistance from the signalman that I made the footbridge in time! *3641/1*

Above Deganwy, Gwynedd; DMU, 15.42 from Llandudno,
7 September 1989.
The rear of the sleepers are also seen receding on the left. *3641/3*

Below The Warren, Llandudno, Gwynedd; DMU,
09.10 Llandudno-Llandudno Junction, 14 October 1981.
I have strayed out of the hotel between breakfast and a first conference
session. It looks as though a storm is brewing. *3646*

Left Llandudno Junction, Gwynedd; DMU, 11.30 Bangor-Manchester (Victoria), 24 October 1980.
The gallows-style signal gives this picture some character, but do note that it is about to be replaced by a colour light with a 'feather' for the Conwy Valley branch. *3657*

Below Gorddinan, Gwynedd; Class 47 No 47827, 13.35 Blaenau Ffestiniog-Llandudno, 7 September 1989.
Having travelled by coach from Bangor to Portmadoc, the travellers on the InterCity special have covered the Ffestiniog Railway and have now settled down to lunch. I saw the train ECS near Dolwyddelan and, apart from staff, only Alan Pegler seemed to be about, and waved at me from an open window. He gave the commentary on these specials, but I wonder if the participants always appreciated the finer railway points of his descriptions. When the train had passed me a French tourist raced up on his cycle. 'When is the next train like that?' 'In about 18 months,' I replied. *3680/1*

Abergele & Pensarn, Clwyd; Class 47 No 47439, 16.17 Llandudno-Crewe, 7 September 1989.
I thought that this train went to Scarborough, and it looks rather long for a short trip, but the timetable does not appear to back me up. It was followed by David Ward's special. This is the area where foot crossings exist between caravan sites – a danger to everyone and a far cry from when they were installed between open fields. *3721 & 3725*

Above Rhyl, Clwyd; Class 47, 11.50 Euston-Holyhead, 20 April 1989.

This was a busy station at summer weekends when holidays were taken from the West Midlands on a fortnightly basis, but quieter now. The signal gantry in the distance bears witness to those bustling days. *3746/5*

Below Talacre, Clwyd; Class 20s, No 20099 leading, coal empties to Point of Ayr colliery, 21 April 1989.

My experience of goods trains is that they rarely run to time, but this one was to the minute. It appeared on the down line from Chester, crossed to the up local and ran into the platform, disused since 1966. The locos ran round and it was off to the colliery in no time. *3749/10*

Reading, Berks; HSTs to and from Paddington, 14 July 1980.
You will already have seen a black and white picture of this scene (page 17), but now here it is in glorious Kodachrome.
As well as the two express trains a DMU is leaving for Redhill. *1616*

Above Restormel Castle, Cornwall; Class 50 No 50023 *Howe*, 06.45 Swindon-Penzance; 21 April 1988.
On page 26 there is a view the other way with the empty newspaper train approaching. *1934*

Below Lostwithiel, Cornwall; HST, 09.33 Penzance-Paddington 'Cornish Riviera Express', 21 April 1988.
In the up siding there is a raft of 'clayhood' wagons available for china clay traffic, which are now obsolete. *1950*

Above Bullingham, Hereford & Worcester; Class 37 No 37430
Cwmbran, 14.00 Cardiff-Crewe, 3 May 1989.
I'm on one of the InterCity Land Cruises, and while most of the
passengers have gone for a tour of the cathedral I decided to walk from
Hereford station to this location and hoped the working would not be
a DMU – and it wasn't! The River Wye is in the foreground. *2928/1*

Below Medlock Vale Viaduct, Greater Manchester; Class 47 No
47422, 11.01 Liverpool (Lime Street)-Newcastle, 17 March 1989.
The coaches are all in the short-lived Trans-Pennine livery and are
between Ashton-under-Lyne and Miles Platting. Equivalent trains
now run via Guide Bridge to Piccadilly. *4685/13*

Conwy Castle, Gwynedd; Class 25, down freight, 14 October 1980.
The tide is in and there are many boats in the estuary. 3626

Above Melton Ross, Humberside; Class 37s, No 37153 leading, iron ore tipplers, 13 May 1982.

This morning I drove from Nawton over the Humber Bridge to show an AV of tourism to Glanford Brigg Council. Now I'm free to visit the railway, hence this picture. 6247

Below Renishaw, South Yorks; Class 37, up oil tanks, 26 August 1981.

Later we shall see a picture taken at Melton Mowbray earlier on this day (page 64). When trains first entered Sheffield from the south they had to run via Rotherham along this line; later the locomotives became more powerful and the route via Bradway Tunnel was opened in 1871. The locomotive is spotless! 5218

Above Lindwell, West Yorks; Class 47, 07.57 Weymouth-Bradford (Exchange) via Barnsley, Huddersfield and Halifax, 19 July 1980. I am above Greetland Junction with Arthur Kinder, and we have walked some distance to reach this location from the south. Squealing out-of-gauge noises prompted a run to the summit as the train was very much on time. *4697*

Left Nafferton, Humberside; 'Pacer' DMUs, Hull-Scarborough, 21 May 1988. The building housing the booking office is at right angles to the line. *6414*

Above Moorcock, North Yorks; Class 47, 16.35 Carlisle-Hull via Leeds, 9 September 1986.
We are on the watershed, right on the boundary with Cumbria, and the roads diverge for Kirkby Stephen, Garsdale and Wensleydale. The chapel is still in use. *8954Z*

Below Invershin, Highland; Class 26 No 26041, JSG special to Wick, 24 April 1982.
I had advised the hotel that we would be going up and down the viaduct after breakfast in case any residents wanted to photograph the event. Some did! It only takes 2 minutes to reach the station at Culrain on the far side of the bridge, but is several miles by road. Hence there is much trespass, and at one time a footpath was proposed within the girders. *11120*

Above Loch Carron, Highland; Class 37 No 37261, 'The Royal Scotsman' from the Kyle, 19 May 1985.
Here it is on the inaugural run, when it was composed of vintage rolling-stock and looked very handsome. *11042*

Below Corrour, Highland; Class 27 No 27106, JSG special to Glenfinnan, 25 April 1981.
What a perfect photo with which to finish the colour section. The Mallaig-Glasgow train approaches. *11310*

3.
MIDLANDS AND THE NORTH

When the Midland had its own route into Bristol via Mangotsfield it was common for trains to terminate in Bristol (Temple Meads). Under BR, trains were diverted at Yate to join the former GWR main line to South Wales, and Bristol Parkway station was created. Since then it has become common for trains on the north-east/south-west axis to continue beyond Bristol on the former Bristol & Exeter route – an obvious improvement for travellers.

At the same time long-distance travellers to and from Shrewsbury have been put at a disadvantage. Whereas in earlier years regular through expresses called there en route from Paddington to Chester/Birkenhead, now DMUs are the order of the day and London passengers have to change at Birmingham or Wolverhampton. I never understood why Euston/Holyhead HSTs could not have been diverted this way. But now there are rumours that a Marylebone/Wrexham service may be introduced. Let's see!

The reconstruction of the Leven Viaduct near Ulverston in 2006 resulted in the termination of passenger trains at Grange-over-Sands. It occurred to me that the nuclear flask trains would also be affected and would have to run via Carlisle instead of the Barrow avoiding line. I estimated that the 15.35 south from Sellafield would have to leave instead at about 14.00. This proved true, but prolonged waits to photograph it at St Bees and at Aspatria (in pouring rain!) were in vain. I did, however, have the luck to see it running southbound near Nethertown and took the rear view.

When BR took over there were various alternative routes between Sheffield and Leeds and there can be little doubt that some rationalisation was due. A picture included here shows an express on the former Midland Railway at Royston & Notton; now such trains run by way of Moorthorpe and the GNER route. At one time main-line trains between Sheffield and York ran through Pontefract, but now these are reduced to two DMUs each way each day. Sometimes the express runs via Wakefield and Leeds to York and at other times via Doncaster. A real corridor of service!

The period of the pictures in this book coincided with real threats to the future of the Settle & Carlisle route, now happily resolved in a positive way. I made a personal objection to the closure and was heard at the Inquiry in Settle late one evening. In his book *The Battle for the Settle & Carlisle*, the late James Towler, Chairman of the TUCC, says that it was the diversity of the submissions that made his three days in Settle so absorbing. 'Among the 70 or so individual objectors who spoke was John Spencer Gilks, one of the country's foremost authorities on railways. He made the novel point that if the Settle-Carlisle line closed, he was not satisfied that the money saved would be spent in a manner equally beneficial to him as a taxpayer.' I have always pointed out that taxpayers in towns deprived of their trains have not had an obvious tax reduction in recognition of the fact.

The associated and older line from Settle Junction now to Carnforth via Borwick was deprived this year of its last working signal box. The signals at Wennington were removed and the box demolished, leaving a stone-faced alcove where it had stood. Who today would create such a quality alcove? Trains can only operate now at 40-minute intervals.

Above Wickwar Tunnel, Avon; Class 45, 07.34 Leeds-Penzance
(1V80), 3 April 1982.

The coach party from the 'Talking of Trains' class at Surbiton are
standing in line on a footpath covering an aqueduct over the former
Midland main line from Derby to Bristol, and must have been a
surprise to the driver when he emerged from the darkness. As you can
see the tunnel is hewn through solid rock and often caused trouble in
past years. *2223*

Below Dunhampstead, Hereford & Worcester; Class 37,
08.24 York-Tenby, 5 July 1980.

My diary simply says 'Gavin' and gives no details of the day's outing.
You can see the Lickey Hills on the horizon. In later years we were to
photograph this train on the Tenby branch itself; the stock then used
to run empty to Swansea. *2624*

Above Moreton-in-Marsh, Glos; Class 50, 16.03 Worcester
(Shrub Hill)-Paddington, 3 April 1982.
Keen readers will note that our coach tour has moved north. The line
is single track from Norton Junction and Evesham to this point, but
then remains double as far as the level crossing at Ascott-under-
Wychwood. Do notice the semaphore signals. In 1965 the class had
travelled on the 13.25 from Oxford, which shunted here to be
overtaken by an express; we then moved on to Honeybourne and
Leamington. *2458*

Below Colwall, Hereford & Worcester; DMU, 17.00 Birmingham
(New Street)-Hereford, 29 July 1982.
I'm on a visit to the Heart of England Tourist Board at Tewkesbury and
came out here in the evening. The building that seems to have been
sliced by the railway is the Free Grammar School, and trains must
shake the foundations. The Malverns crown the horizon. *2507*

Above Ryecroft Junction, West Midlands; Class 37 No 37158, breakdown train, 8 February 1988.

We are now in an industrial area for a change, on the outskirts of Walsall. I stayed last night at Tixall Gatehouse near Stafford, and I'm making my way to Tonbridge in Kent. These pictures are taken around lunchtime. The train has come from Water Orton via the line through Sutton Park, which lost its regular passenger service in 1965. The junction is with the former routes from Lichfield and from Wolverhampton. The railway to Rugeley had just been re-opened for passengers to Hednesford – hence my visit – and these trains now run again to the West Coast Main Line and Stafford. *4974*

Below Ryecroft Junction, West Midlands; Class 37 No 37519, up strip steel, 8 February 1988.

I'm eating my sandwiches and, to my delight, trains keep coming by. A little road runs parallel to the line and there is room to park. *4977*

Above Preston, Salop; Class 47, 11.33 Shrewsbury-Euston, 5 May 1988.

I'm on my way to Llanfair Waterdine and, yet again, it's time for a sandwich lunch. This was a really quiet place then, but now a motorway runs immediately to the left of the photo and I pause here no more. Shrewsbury is on the horizon, a place with no direct train to London these days. Why don't they divert the Holyhead service this way? The locomotive is in Network SouthEast colours. *2760*

Below Shrewsbury, Salop; Class 25 No 25192, ballast empties to Llynclys, 18 April 1985.

Gavin and I have come here to photograph the period signalling equipment and boxes for the Friends of the National Railway Museum, and stay at The Lion. Merrick Roocroft is our host, and Derek and Stuart the men at work in the famous Severn Bridge signal box, from which this view is taken, looking east. People could not have been more helpful. The spur on the right avoids the station and was used by holiday trains, which sometimes waited there in the early hours pending signalmen coming on duty on the Cambrian route. *2761*

Left Woofferton, Hereford & Worcester;
Class 37, southbound waste disposal,
21 November 1987.
Until 1961 this was the junction for Tenbury
Wells and Kidderminster, the track diverging
right between the goods shed and the signal
box. I'm using a car hired for the weekend
under the InterCity Interlude scheme, which
lasted but a short time because of its financial
losses. The ticket enabled me to travel
between York and Worcester 1st Class (only
this did not exist south of Birmingham), pick
up the car and spend the weekend at the Elms
Hotel at Abberley. Here I was welcomed by
the manager with a bouquet of flowers and a
bottle of champagne and advised that
complimentary sherry was in my bedroom
with two glasses. Michael Whitehouse joined
me for dinner. It was an excellent
arrangement while it lasted! I cannot find any
reference to the scheme in *The InterCity Story*
(Oxford Publishing Co, 1994), which
otherwise is a fine record of BR's notable
achievements. *2907*

Below Offa's Dyke, Hereford & Worcester/Gwent; Class 47,
southbound oil tanks, 14 June 1988.
I'm just north of Llanfihangel Crucorney at the summit of the line and
the hills surrounding Pontrilas are on the horizon. The crop has been
harvested early. While Beeching had in mind to downgrade this line,
and diverted the through expresses via Birmingham, it has seen a
revival and has a better passenger service than hitherto. I have driven
over from Presteigne. *2939*

Above Haughton, Salop; Class 37 No 37429 *Eisteddfod Genedlaethol*, northbound oil tanks, 16 June 1988.

When I came across the loops and (switched-out) signal box (behind the camera) in the depths of the country I could hardly believe my eyes. And by good fortune there is a succession of freight trains. My route is from Llanarman Dyffryn Ceiriog (Hand Hotel) to Matlock Bath (New Bath Hotel), which is an interesting journey. *2774*

Below Prees, Salop; DMU, 13.50 Crewe-Shrewsbury, 16 June 1988.

A delightful survival in rural country, the station here still has a signal box, level crossing and semaphore signals (as far as I know). I'm a little nearer Matlock. *4040*

Above Rugeley, Staffs; Class 20s, southbound coal, 8 February 1988.
This train was on the up slow line of the West Coast Main Line and has zigzagged right across to gain the tracks to Ryecroft Junction at Walsall, though whether it will go that far I do not know. *4013*

Below Worleston, Ches; Class 47, westbound tanks, 27 June 1981.
This weekend, based at Audlem, involved 510 miles of motoring. I was met by Gavin at Nuneaton as I travelled there on the 18.05 from Euston in the diner. In later years I was to visit this line on many occasions to see the Class 37s on passenger turns. The Euston/Holyhead trains are still of interest. *4055*

Above Helsby, Ches; Class 31 Nos 31185 (leading) and 31181, tanks to Ellesmere Port, exact date unknown.

The tracks above the locomotives run from Warrington to Chester and carry the service from Manchester to the North Wales coast. The five trains (MF) on the branch originate at Helsby and seem intended to serve workmen and schoolchildren; passengers at Ince & Elton should be certain of the schedule, otherwise a lengthy wait will ensue. On Saturdays there are two bus journeys at the oddest times. *4070*

Below Rufford, Lancs; DMU, 11.44 Ormskirk-Preston, 29 May 1984.

This used to be the main line from Liverpool, and express trains to Glasgow/Edinburgh regularly came this way at high speed. No longer – today the trains terminate at Ormskirk from where, after a walk along the common platform, the electric Metro is taken into the city. It is a single line now too, but with a loop at Rufford. *9183*

Above **Kirkham, Lancs; Class 47, 08.55 Euston-Blackpool North, 5 September 1981.**
As you can see by the 'feathers' on the signals, this is the junction for Lytham and Blackpool South. It also used to be the junction for the direct line to Blackpool, but this has been replaced by the M55, traffic from which regularly blocks the southbound M6 late on Sunday afternoon, just as the trains queued up to gain the main line at Preston in the old days. I was running a transport conference in the Imperial Hotel, Blackpool, in March 1982 when Sir Peter Parker, in an adjoining private room, was said to have promised the Council electric trains to London. But it was not to be. 9263

Left **Weeton, Lancs; DMU, 12.44 Blackpool North-Manchester (Victoria), 5 September 1981.**
You can see the neglect of existing facilities by the condition of this box. What must it have been like inside? It was brought into use on days of peak traffic. I know not whether it still exists but I do know that Railtrack deserve credit for the overhaul and improvement of such structures –double-glazing, for instance. 9274

Above Ashton-under-Lyne, Greater Manchester; Class 47 No 47444,
14.20 Newcastle-Liverpool (Lime Street), 17 March 1989.
This train is at least 2 hours late due to engine failure, and Arthur
Kinder and I had written it off when suddenly it appeared here. We are
taking pictures between Stalybridge and Miles Platting in anticipation
of the transfer of the trains from Victoria to Piccadilly stations, thus via
Guide Bridge (where the 15mph restriction of yore has still not been
eased to my knowledge). 4685/3

Below Miles Platting, Greater Manchester; Class 47,
09.01 Liverpool (Lime Street)-Newcastle, 17 March 1989.
This train has just climbed the 1 in 59 (later 1 in 47) incline from
Victoria and is diverging from the line to Rochdale, which it will rejoin
at Heaton Lodge Junction beyond Huddersfield. 4685/32

Above Manchester (Oxford Road), Greater Manchester; Class 47 No 47380, southbound oil tanks, and EMU No 304 009 to Alderley Edge via Styal, 17 March 1989.
There is really nothing to add! *9193*

Below Mouldsworth, Ches; DMU, 09.28 Chester-Manchester (Oxford Road), 8 July 1987.
These trains now change their route at Altrincham and terminate at Piccadilly via Northenden and Stockport. Until 1991 there was a connection from Mouldsworth to West Cheshire Junction near Ellesmere Port. *4089*

Bescar Lane, Lancs; DMU, 15.25 Southport-York, 29 May 1984. I'm spending ten days at my then favourite retreat – Close House Farm, Giggleswick – and have come into this low-lying plain of West Lancashire crossed in almost a straight line for some dozen miles by the former Lancashire & Yorkshire Railway. Businessmen in Manchester used 'club cars' on their commuter trains from Blackpool, Llandudno and Windermere, and I thought from Southport too, but can find no formal reference to back this up. This train ran to York for only a short time. The stations at Bescar Lane and New Lane serve very rural communities and seem to have been forgotten. 9228

Above Foxfield (Duddon sands), Cumbria; DMU,
11.43 Lancaster-Millom, 25 May 1987.
The Distant signal warns of the approach to Foxfield across the
viaduct. This is a fascinating area where the sheep are said still to be
radioactive from the Chernobyl nuclear disaster. The turf is beautifully
soft and the air fresh and lovely. 9553

Below Parton, Cumbria; DMU, 10.35 Carlisle-Whitehaven
(Bransty), 26 September 1988.
The coastline has turned from south- to west-facing and the view is to
the hills of Galloway (behind the camera). During the reconstruction
of the Leven Viaduct at Ulverston in 2006 the nuclear flask trains had
to reach the West Coast Main Line via Carlisle and came through
here. 9656

Above **Wellingborough (Finedon Rd), Northants; Class 45, 07.58 Leeds-St Pancras, 12 July 1980.**
The Midland main line tends to run in the middle of a valley, and intermediate bridges take a long time to reach by car from one to the next. It was just north of here that I saw the down Manchester (Blue) Pullman for the first time and was struck by its speed. This train will be slowing to the curve through the station. *4882*

Right **Ellistown, Leics; Class 56, 'merry-go-round' coal empties, 16 June 1983.**
I seem to have one photograph only on the Leicester-Burton line, and even the precise date is a little suspect. Bardon quarries provide much of the traffic in the form of roadstone. Regular passenger trains were withdrawn in 1964, but on 27 September 1969 I chartered a special (with a WR 'InterCity' unit) this way from Clapham Junction to Derby, calling at Harrow on the Hill, Quainton Road and Clipston & Oxenden. The driver advised me that there was some doubt about the use of this route, but at Knighton Junction we were signalled this way, so all was well! *4941*

Above **Melton Mowbray, Leics; Class 25, up parcels,
26 August 1981.**
For some reason I had left home in Kingston at 5.20am and had
breakfast at The Haycock at Wansford before going on to Trowell
Junction and Dunford Bridge. It was glorious weather. I've always had
a soft spot for Melton Mowbray, having spent several very happy
weekends there at the turn of the 1950s/'60s looking at the joint line
with Geoff Hunt and the trains to/from Leicester (Belgrave Road).
4926

Below **Trowell Junction, Notts; Class 47 No 47532,
07.17 Harwich (Parkeston Quay)-Manchester (Piccadilly)
'The North Country Continental', 26 August 1981.**
This train has great significance for me as it carried me as a National
Service airman on 29 April 1952 from Bury St Edmunds to Manchester
to join a course on which I met Hugh Davies and began the railway
interest that has led to this book! In the picture it carries two buffet
cars for some reason. When I travelled it used the Sykes Junction-
Clarborough route to cross the Trent and took the Woodhead route
over the Pennines. My diary records 'quiet March, lovely tulips at
Spalding, smoky Sheffield'. By now it is travelling via Peterborough,
Nottingham and the Hope Valley. *5104*

Above Sheffield (Midland), South Yorks; Class 45, 16.19 from
St Pancras, and two DMUs, 17 July 1980.
I am about to join an RCTS special to climb Worsborough Bank for the
last time. It was a memorable evening. *5201*

Below Royston & Notton, South Yorks; Class 47, 06.55 Glasgow
(Central)-Nottingham (Midland), 30 May 1981.
This is the old Midland main line from Sheffield to Leeds, which is
about to be downgraded – the passenger traffic will be diverted via
Moorthorpe, then the 'fast' lines will be lifted. It so happened that on
Sunday my York-Birmingham HST was diverted this way (and via
Lichfield) – a bonus. *5228*

Above Skipton, North Yorks; Class 47, 11.50 Glasgow (Central)-Nottingham (Midland), and two Class 31s, Tilcon train (Swinden-Hull) in siding, 4 September 1981.

Plans are afoot to close the Settle & Carlisle line and the London connection has been cut; later it will be diverted over Shap. But the powers that be did not expect the late James Towler to chair the local TUCC as effectively as he did. The media loved it. Was it the Rt Hon William Whitelaw, Lady Thatcher's right-hand man – whose constituency just touched the line – who persuaded her to save it? *8303*

Below Settle Junction, North Yorks; Class 31, down ballast train, 31 May 1984.

This has become quite a famous spot in English folklore, but ease of access is not as simple as it was at one time. When Prince Charles was to join the Royal Train at Settle to go to Kirkby Stephen and Appleby we knew that it would be held at the junction until he was on the station platform. We drove away as it started off, but even with a sprint along the bypass we were hard put to reach Helwith Bridge in advance. We did and the smoke screen produced by *Duchess of Sutherland* needed to be seen to be believed! *8454*

Above Clapham, North Yorks; DMU, 15.32 Lancaster-Hull, 31 March 1984.

This was during a round-trip of 145 miles, based at Giggleswick and including the Garsdale end of Rise Hill Tunnel and Appleby, with a fast run on the M6 southbound. This was the Clapham Junction of the north until 1966, and you can see how the train comes round to join the direct route. The last local passenger trains ran in 1954. In latter years the goods came from Tebay three times per week and we used it on 30 May 1960. It shunted at Sedbergh but there was no other traffic and we reached here so soon that we were able to join an earlier train to Carnforth. 8569

Below Capernwray Viaduct, Lancs; DMU, 12.16 Morecambe-Leeds, 28 May 1983.

These Trans-Pennine units were employed on the line just before their withdrawal from service. Earlier that day we had seen *City of Wells* head a special here. 8625

Left Langcliffe, North Yorks; Class 45, 11.50 Glasgow (Central)-Nottingham (Midland), 6 April 1981.
We now start our pictures of the Settle & Carlisle line, and you can see in the background how the line had to turn to avoid high ground and enter Stainforth Tunnel. 8685

Below Helwith Bridge, North Yorks; Class 47 No 47569, return Appleby-Yarmouth excursion, 31 March 1984.
During the threat of closure to the S&C many excursions were run from various parts of the country, but I think this must have been one of the longer outings. It is past six o'clock already and there are many miles to go. 8709

Right Salt Lake City, North Yorks; Class 47, 10.40 Carlisle-Leeds, 9 September 1986.
This was one of a number of terraces of cottages built by the Midland Railway to house their signalmen and platelayers. These tiny communities had a character all their own. 8750

Below right Blea Moor, North Yorks; preserved Class 40 No D200, 10.40 Carlisle-Leeds, 14 November 1983.
Closure is really in the air now and the passenger service has been reduced to two trains each way composed of just four coaches. The signal box is in the background and the outlook is bleak in more senses than one. 8795

Above **Blea Moor Tunnel (north end), Cumbria; Class 47, 15.55 Leeds-Carlisle, 30 March 1984.**
Our track permits are coming in useful now, allowing Gavin and myself to walk the track from here to the mouth of Rise Hill Tunnel (excluding the viaducts). In talking to a ganger we learned that maintenance had been reduced in 1968; in practice the government grants had been shifted to the urban areas where there were more votes. *8820*

Below **Arten Gill Viaduct, Cumbria; Class 47 No 47588, 'The Pennine Limited', 9 September 1986.**
Here is another of David Ward's specials heading north. Well turned out! *8880*

Dent Dale, Cumbria; DMU, 11.02 Leeds-Carlisle, 9 September 1986.
This picture indicates quite dramatically how the S&C cuts across the grain of the land and provides splendid views in good weather. 8883

Above left Rise Hill, Cumbria; Class 47 No 47533,
10.40 Carlisle-Leeds, 31 March 1984.
The train is about to leave Garsdale, enter the tunnel and emerge in
Ribblesdale. To get to this point we have climbed from the Sedbergh-
Hawes road to what I have come to know as 'coronary bridge'. Notice
the snow on the distant fells. *8927*

Left Lunds, North Yorks; Class 47, 15.55 Leeds-Carlisle,
9 June 1984.
A viaduct is preceded by Moorcock Tunnel, then the train enters
Upper Wensleydale with the summit soon at Ais Gill. Although the
timetable suggests this train, I am a little suspicious because of its
length, but it is a Saturday. *8954AC*

Above Mallerstang, Cumbria; Class 47 No 47283, 15.55 Leeds-
Carlisle, precise date uncertain.
We're on the descent now and it takes time and effort to reach this west
side of the line, but it is worth the trouble in the afternoon. When I
visited the nearby signal box the wet fields damaged the soles of my
shoes. *8954CA*

Right Crowdundle Viaduct, Cumbria; Class 47, 13.02 Leeds-
Carlisle, 27 May 1989.
We're well north now in the Eden Valley and the parapets of the
viaduct are below us. I'm standing on the highest bridge over the line,
which carries but a farm track and seems out of proportion. I walked to
the right downhill and passed beneath the arch to regain the car about
a mile away. *9065*

Above **Little Salkeld, Cumbria; Class 47 No 47537, 08.25 Leeds-Carlisle, 23 March, 1988.**
I'm returning home from the Farlam Hall Hotel at Hallbankgate – my favourite – and stop to watch the train cross the Briggie Beck by the farm. It is fascinating to compare the viaduct with the tiny bridge on the adjacent road. *9087*

Below **Long Meg, Cumbria; Class 47, 09.25 Carlisle-Euston, 11 December 1983.**
It is a bitterly cold Sunday morning and the trains are being diverted from the West Coast Main Line. These sidings from a nearby quarry used to originate anhydrite trains to Widnes, but as you can see they are out of use (and lifted now?). *9093*

Above **Eden Lacey Viaduct, Cumbria; Class 47 No 47471, 16.15 Carlisle-Leeds, 22 September 1988.**
Just beyond Long Meg is this viaduct, glowing in the evening sunshine. *9104*

Below **Armathwaite, Cumbria; Class 31, 16.35 Carlisle-Leeds, 5 August 1983.**
Gavin with his camera and tripod is in the foreground. This is our second visit here because first time I was guilty of failing to watch the clock and enjoyed an ice-cream too much. I still got my picture but he was unable to frame his to his satisfaction. Thus end the pictures of the Settle & Carlisle – but it is still there for your attention. *9134*

4.
THE EAST

As I write this (4 November 2006) the largest freighter in the world is due to dock at Felixstowe with containers of Chinese Christmas presents – it is a quarter of a mile in length. No wonder that the branch from Westerfield (Ipswich) is due for expansion to accommodate more freight traffic. Indeed, the line westward, including Nuneaton, is being upgraded and conflict with the West Coast Main Line avoided. The passenger service between Peterborough and Birmingham is probably better than ever before. But trains such as 'The North Country Continental' (Harwich-Manchester/ Liverpool), which started in 1885, are no more, and there seem to be fewer through services from that port to the west. Presumably more people go abroad by air, but if the global warming precautions are to be meaningful this might change.

Since the 1980s electrification has brought London within easier reach of both Norwich and King's Lynn – my pictures here look quite archival. On the other hand Grimsby and Cleethorpes have seen the loss of London services, and a journey west with a change at Doncaster or Newark is inevitable unless you drive south to Peterborough.

The South Yorkshire Joint Line originally brought together the Great Central, Great Northern, Lancashire & Yorkshire, Midland and North Eastern Railways. It now carries freight from Brancliff East Junction (between Worksop and Sheffield) and either Doncaster or Kirk Sandall (between Doncaster and Stainforth), depending on the route from St Catherine's Junction. Regular traffic is industrial sand from Middleton Towers near King's Lynn. Passenger traffic on the line is rare and a couple of pictures of excursions are included below (pages 86 and 87).

Two closures are still discussed: York-Hull via Pocklington, Market Weighton and Beverley, and the Woodhead route from Sheffield to Manchester, modernised and electrified (DC) as late as 1954. The first would now be a bonus to commuters who find it hard to park in York, for example, while the latter might have taken traffic off the cross-Pennine roads, which the M62 has done for a while but now becomes congested at the slightest provocation.

The Wearhead line from Bishop Auckland to Eastgate has re-opened in part as a preservation route, having closed for months due to financial problems. The TV programme *Look North* has just showed a locomotive on the A1 en route to Wolsingham in time for 'Santa Specials'. When locos have to be taken by lorry is it because transport by rail is too dear or because by road is too cheap? It is thought by the local authorities involved that the railway could be the lifeline to folk in a valley in need of employment following the closure of the cement works. This stratagem has worked elsewhere, so let's watch Weardale in future with hope. Tourism is the key to success.

Above right **Wrabness, Essex; Class 37, 09.40 Liverpool Street-Harwich (Parkeston Quay) 'The Day Continental',**
22 March 1980.
This is the third stop on the 'Talking of Trains' coach tour and we stayed some time due to the number of passing freights from the docks. The next few pictures are taken on the same days in March. We then turn to the 1981 tour on the equivalent Saturday. This picture has that misty East Anglian look. *5656*

Right **Westerfield, Suffolk; DMU, 10.50 Lowestoft-Ipswich,**
22 March 1980.
This is the junction for Felixstowe, which has become more important with the growth of container traffic from the expanding port. The Beeching Report (page 105) recommended closure of the East Suffolk line (Westerfield-Yarmouth South Town) and his henchman at York – Margetts – fought Gerry Fiennes, the GM Eastern Region, who suggested a way for its retention. The line is still there, though single track, and a London service has been restored from Lowestoft. Incidentally, Marples, the Minister who received Beeching's recommendations, was said to be furious at the detailed list of line and station closures in the report. This came from a scientist, not a politician! *5719*

Above Diss, Norfolk; Class 47, 14.29 Norwich-Liverpool Street, 22 March 1980.
It is a really straight main line, and since this picture was taken electrification has taken place; London can now be reached in an hour from Ipswich, and there are daily commuters from here. *5710*

Below Great Chesterford, Essex; Class 31, 17.36 Liverpool Street-Cambridge, 22 March 1980.
Electrification has since taken place here, too – from London to King's Lynn – which has enhanced property values and facilitated the growth of Stansted Airport. It is a far cry from the three years (1848-51) when it was the junction for Newmarket. *5573*

Above Chippenham Junction, Cambs; DMU, 16.12 Cambridge-Ipswich, 22 March 1980.

This was an inaccessible place but worth the walk through the woods, provided one takes care if racehorse training is in progress. It is a potentially misleading place-name, and is where the trains from Ipswich to Cambridge part company with those to Ely and the north. 5680

Below Soham, Cambs; Class 31, 16.42 Peterborough-Harwich (Parkeston Quay), 21 March 1981.

Soham is a place of sadness in recent years and of bravery during the Second World War when a truck of explosives was detached from a burning train, but before it could be shunted into open countryside it exploded, bringing death and much destruction to property. 5696

Above Eccles Road, Norfolk; Class 25, 15.18 Norwich-Birmingham (New Street), 22 March 1980.
The 'Talking of Trains' class spent a jolly time in and out of the signal box here while the trains came and went. For a while a siding existed for A11 road improvements. 5866

Below Ely North Junction, Cambs; Class 31 No 31226, 16.00 King's Lynn-Liverpool Street, 21 March 1981.
You may recall from earlier books that to photograph this location where lines come together from King's Lynn, March and Norwich we travelled by plane from Biggin Hill to Radcliffe-on-Trent. This time a simple coach trip suffices. 5888

Above **French Drove & Gedney Hill, Lincs; DMU, 14.45 March-Doncaster, 21 March 1981.**
We are really in the wilds here at a station that closed to passengers in 1961 and to freight in 1964, having received its double-barrelled name in 1938. We so timed our coach visit that the local trains passed at this point, which gave the signalman (whose box we invaded) and District Inspector something to talk about. There used to be loops north of here for freight to be overtaken. On the face of it this route was dispensable, but as freight traffic from the East to the North expands GNER will find congestion a problem at Peterborough, especially if it needs to cross over to go via Spalding. 5958

Below **Skegness, Lincs; Class 47s and DMU laying over, 29 August 1988.**
When Barbara Castle was Minister of Transport she recalled the importance of trains to Blackpool for Wakes Weeks and was determined that Skegness, the resort of the East Midlands, should be spared closure for the same reason. And so it was. 6069

Above Hubbert's Bridge, Lincs; Class 20s, No 20075 leading,
09.22 Derby–Skegness, 20 June 1981.

Indeed, some holiday trains had unusual motive power to ensure that
they provided due capacity. The signalman here has an unenviable
task: from the left the road comes across a narrow bridge, while on the
right there is an immediate cross-roads with the A1122 and no space
to park by the gates. He has to open these by hand, so there is plenty
opportunity for verbal abuse. 6005

Below Hubbert's Bridge, Lincs; Class 45, Freightliner from
Boston, 20 June 1981.

In addition, the double track becomes single here, so tablet exchanges
delay matters even more. Currently a train leaves the docks at 14.19 for
Mountsorrel on Tuesdays and Fridays and at 16.43 for Toton when
required on Wednesdays. 6007

Above King's Cross, Greater London; HST, 08.30 from
Newcastle Central, 22 April 1980.
So the paraphernalia of modern signalling and electrification has
arrived, and a journey by what is today GNER with its dining cars is
probably the best in the country. *5330*

Below Stamford, Lincs; Class 31, 09.41 Norwich-Birmingham
(New Street), 21 March 1981.
More and more traffic comes this way, much from Felixstowe, and work
at Nuneaton will facilitate its movement over the West Coast Main
Line into the Midlands and beyond. Quite an ecclesiastical scene!
3927

Above Lowfield, Notts; Class 56 No 56113, Colwick-Immingham oil tanks, 21 August 1986.
Signalman John Collins has just received the token for the single track from Bottesford West Junction on all that remains of the joint line from Welham Junction (near Market Harborough) via Melton Mowbray. Crossing my favourite High Leicestershire, I only travelled it once (to Nottingham) on an RCTS special that played the role of express and had to hang about at Saxondale Junction, killing time – ridiculous! 3978

Below Newark (Northgate), Notts; Class 47 No 47341, Immingham-Colwick oil tanks, 21 August 1986.
Here is the equivalent southbound train leaving the East Coast Main Line, as the masts are being put up in readiness for electrification. 3984

Above Lincoln, Pelham Street Junction, Lincs; Class 33
No 31125, freight from Boston via Sleaford, 10 October 1984.
The crossovers no longer exist as the tracks to the right to St Mark's station have been lifted. When I used 'The North Country Continental' (see page 76 above) I was seated near the back of the train and could see the locomotive approaching the then level crossing gates with great caution as they were not opened to trains until the last minute so as not to congest the city streets too much. *6135*

Below Woodhouse, South Yorks; DMU, 17.54 Sheffield (Midland)-March, 12 September 1981.
Earlier in the day I had tried without success to meet friends aboard a narrow-boat on the Trent & Mersey Canal. This unit has a long way to go. Nearby the 'real' Great Central Railway set out for London. *4382*

Above Maltby, South Yorks; Class 47 No 47631, Doncaster-King's Cross special, 1 March 1986.
Gavin Morrison has kindly brought me here and received a load of abuse from the signalman for his trouble! Perhaps he had had to miss a football match. There can be few occasions when Pullman cars have come this way on the South Yorkshire Joint Line. David Ward is in charge. *4372*

Below Applehurst Junction, South Yorks; Class 47 No 47659, 07.55 St Pancras 'The Aardvark and Clown' special, 30 August 1988.
Another David Ward special, this one covered a circuit from Pye Bridge Junction on the Midland Erewash Valley Line (left 10.09am, returned 6.29pm) outward via Mansfield and return via the Foxlow Junction/Elmton & Cresswell line. It is a Tuesday. I have trespassed, and unknown to me the train is held at Joan Croft Junction while I walk beside the track towards Adwick Junction as far as the bridge over the East Coast Main Line. Had I known I would have photographed it from there too. *6220*

Brookhouse, South Yorks; Class 47 No 47659, 07.55 St Pancras 'The Aardvark and Clown' special, 30 August 1988. The South Yorkshire Joint Line runs through remote countryside from Brancliffe East Junction (on the Sheffield-Retford section) to St Catherine's Junction for Doncaster or Kirk Sandal (on the Doncaster-Hull/Grimsby section), where the industrial sand train from Middleton Towers comes to an end at Rockware Glass. 4365

Above Cleethorpes, Humberside; DMU, 11.30 to Doncaster, 15 February 1985.

This is the only occasion when, due to roadworks, I held up the men assigned to look after me. Although understandably annoyed at the delay, they still led me up the signal gantries from which I could take views. I loathe those ladders! *6330*

Below Goole Swing Bridge, Humberside; Class 45, 09.41 Manchester (Piccadilly)-Hull, 29 July 1984.

When I retired and set up Ryedale Audio-Visual Enterprise Ltd, we were asked by BR to record the working of this bridge over the River Ouse, as it was anticipated that the line would be shut between Goole and Staddlethorpe. In fact this has not occurred. Signalman George Lee was our helpful guide and we made several visits. Some of the working gear was dated 1868, yet the span can turn within 1 minute. The bridge had to stay open to river traffic over Christmas when BR closed down, and because there was no way off the pontoon George spent a happy time watching the wildlife. *5460*

Above Selby, North Yorks; HST, 07.15 Edinburgh (Waverley)-
King's Cross, 19 May 1980.

My diary records that this was a very hot day and that I had come to
look at work on the diversionary route round the new coalfield (already
shut). Selby remains on the Leeds-Hull route it was built to serve (the
original terminus visible above the second coach), and Hull Trains
come this way to Doncaster and London. *5507*

Below Escrick, North Yorks; Class 31, down freight,
19 May 1980.

Our visit was also to picture the line that was to be closed, and this
view and the next come from the set. North of here a cycleway has
been created; to the south the A19 has taken over the trackbed. *5527*

Above Bishopthorpe, North Yorks; Class 55 'Deltic', Edinburgh (Waverley)-King's Cross, June 1981.
The railway has its own swing bridge over the River Ouse at Naburn, but I have had to drive round to get to this viewpoint. Trains no longer run here. *5535*

Below Barrow Hill, Derbys; Class 20s, No 20031 leading, empty hoppers, 26 August 1981.
The sort of industrial scene is rapidly disappearing from the landscape hereabouts – and not too soon! We are on the Foxlow Junction-Elmton & Cresswell line, now lifted I believe. When I chartered the GM(ER) Saloon across here we had to wait at Elmton for another special to vacate the line, so popular was it at the time for enthusiasts. *5122*

Above **Ackworth, West Yorks; Class 47, down tanks, 30 July 1988.**
We are south of Pontefract on a line that sees only two daily local passenger trains each way and one non-stop Virgin 'Voyager'. But until the express trains were diverted via Doncaster or Leeds/Wakefield it was very busy, and is the shortest way from York to Sheffield (the Swinton & Knottingley Joint Line). 4585

Below **Burton Salmon Junction, North Yorks; Class 20s, No 20133 nearest the camera, up freight, 28 May 1982.**
This junction between the original line to York (via Castleford ahead) and that from Pontefract has disappeared and the point of divergence is at Milford Junction, just a short way to the north. 4579

Left Sherburn Junction, North Yorks; DMU, 15.25 York-Hull, 17 May 1982.
This service can run either via Hambleton North Curve, created with the Selby Diversion, or by the older line here, thus calling at Church Fenton and Sherburn-in-Elmet and ending at Gascoigne Wood. I'm on a disused footpath. *4566*

Below left Chaloner's Whin Junction, North Yorks; Class 45 No 45111 *Grenadier Guardsman*, 08.15 Newcastle Central-Liverpool (Lime Street), June 1981.
This is the place just on the southern outskirts of York where the ECML used to diverge to serve Selby before continuing south. Now it's the site of a Tesco supermarket and the trains turn south further on at Colton Junction. *4540*

Right York, North Yorks; DMUs to Harrogate and Scarborough, 24 May 1980.
It's 08.48 and I'm joining the Manchester train heading for the Rainhill Cavalcade – quite an unusual day. Since then the platforms have been renumbered and the track has been lifted under the right-hand train, as it were. *6916*

Below The roller-blind departure indicator at York on 23 February 1984. *6904*

Below right Ilkley, West Yorks; prototype Class 140 DMU, June 1981.
This is the highlight of a press trip from Leeds, and Peter Keen is about to give us a pep talk about this new unit. It was the only one of its type and improvements followed. *8276*

Lockwood, West Yorks; DMU, 10.34 Huddersfield-Sheffield (Midland) via Thurgoland, 26 August 1981. The line here has been reduced to a single track but the fine viaduct remains. Trains no longer use the former Great Central route from Penistone but run instead via Barnsley. 4529

Above Near Penistone, West Yorks; DMU, 15.40 Sheffield
(Midland)-Huddersfield, 26 August 1981.
In order to reach the Midland station trains reversed to Nunnery Main
Line Junction. *4403*

Below Strensall, North Yorks; Class 31, 15.57 Scarborough-
Liverpool (Lime Street), 24 July 1984.
There has been a new footbridge here for some years, but the proposed
station fails to materialise. The original station closed in 1930 as buses
drew away local people. *6492*

Above Glaisdale, North Yorks; DMU, 16.11 Whitby-Middlesbrough, 7 April 1980.

It's Easter Monday, so there are no schoolchildren on this working, which is provided mainly for them to return home from schools in Whitby, coaches being unable to negotiate Limber Hill. 6809

Below Battersby, North Yorks; Class 31 No 31299, freight to Whitby, 6 April 1983.

This is the penultimate freight to Whitby. I really like this picture and have explained the circumstances at the beginning of this book. Behind me there is a North Eastern Railway fixed Distant signal, and Battersby still has a working box. Trains have reversed here since 1958. 6869

Above Bishophouse Junction, North Yorks; DMU, 17.12 York-Darlington, 30 May 1980.
The official closing day of the line behind this train, which ran to Coxwold, Kirkbymoorside and Malton and served the village in which I now reside, was 10 August 1964. I often wonder what it would be like if we still had a service to York, and expect that we would have become a commuter village rather than a happy community with many folk working locally. Do notice the White Horse on the distant hills. *7028*

Below Pilmoor, North Yorks; Class 37, up tanks, 30 May 1980.
I went on to picture this train near Sessay Junction with the north side of the triangle for Malton. The signals indicate that crossovers survive. *7037*

Dalton, North Yorks; Class 40, down freight, 30 May 1980.
I'm glad I drove on because this train is a must and the sort we may not witness again in this age of fixed formations.
There is everything here and I suggest you study the view with care! 7046

Above Thirsk, North Yorks; Class 45 No 45134, 08.15 Newcastle Central-Bangor, May 1984.
As a Director of National Transport Tokens Ltd, I used to enjoy travelling 1st Class in these trains to Manchester – normally I had a compartment to myself. The main-line platforms were taken out of use when trains began to sweep through at 125mph. Today most trains here link Middlesbrough and Manchester Airport. *7054*

Below Fishburn Junction, Co Durham; HST, 09.35 Edinburgh-King's Cross, 13 May 1984.
This location is between Ferryhill and Sedgefield, and we have turned off the nearby A1 on our return from my special from Alnmouth to Kilmarnock. It is a Sunday and East Coast Main Line diversions are in operation. The junction was for National Smokeless Fuels' private siding. *7246*

Above Stanhope, Co Durham; Class 37, empties to Eastgate, 18 September 1987.

When the cement works was established in Weardale the planning consent is said to have stipulated the use of rail for works traffic, but as the years went by this was less enforced and the trains stopped running while the road became congested. Now the works has closed but the railway is attempting to re-open to passengers. 7533

Below Relly Mill, Co Durham; Class 40, 17.25 Edinburgh-Liverpool (Lime Street), 23 June 1980.

It is hard to believe that a series of junctions used to lie in the foreground, particularly south to Bishop Auckland and north-west to Consett via Lanchester. In the morning I have given a professional address at Captain Cook's Museum. I returned to London by Motorail from Newcastle. 7604

Above Dilston Crossing, Northumberland; Class 31, eastbound household rubbish, 7 August 1981.

I've travelled Motorail – again – to Newcastle and now I'm making my way to Farlam Hall at Hallbankgate. To do this I turn north here and reconnoitre the former Border Counties line until I come upon the 'Waverley' route – a wonderful journey through superb scenery. But why no longer any trains? 7638

Below Haltwhistle, Northumberland; DMU, 10.43 Carlisle-Newcastle, 24 April 1984.

I'm spending my birthday (52) alone but enjoying every minute in this lovely area. The bus is replacing the branch to Alston. 7662

Above **Brampton Fell, Cumbria; Class 47 No 47645, 16.30 Newcastle-Carlisle, 22 March 1988.**
These short trains were made up to fill in until new DMUs arrived to operate the service. There are hourly trains on this line and short workings to Hexham. *7765*

Below **Gelt Viaduct, Cumbria; Class 47 No 47629, 10.48 Carlisle-Newcastle, 22 March 1988.**
Earlier in the day I visited this spot where stood a beer house (no longer licensed) beside a viaduct with engravings in Latin and English declaring it to be the work of Francis Giles in 1834. *7790*

Above **Alnmouth, Northumberland; Class 47, 00.05 King's Cross-Edinburgh, 12 May 1984.**
This is the sleeper from London, which dallies in Newcastle and then becomes a semi-fast northwards. It is bringing members of the 'Talking of Trains' class from Surbiton, who will be alighting here and joining my special to Kilmarnock currently waiting nearby in the Wooden Bridge Loop. I can smell breakfast cooking! We are going to North Berwick, Dunfermline, Largs and Stranraer. 8007

Right **Chathill, Northumberland; DMU, 17.15 Newcastle-Berwick, 10 June 1986.**
The Post Bus is waiting to take passengers to Bamburgh. When John Wylde was transport co-ordinating officer for Northumberland County Council he couldn't understand why on Saturdays – when United Automobile had a licence to run this service – it failed to connect with the train. He soon discovered that it was a different driver every week and that he had not been advised of the condition. Such is centralisation! The train now terminates here, but has to run forward empty to the loop at Belford before it can cross to the up line. 8055

5.
SCOTLAND

Since devolution of much government administration to Scotland and its control from Edinburgh there has been a resurgent interest in railways. Much of this devolves around the capital city, and work has already been done and is in progress. Now authority has been given to restore the former 'Waverley' route as far as Galashiels, and I await developments with interest.

It was in anticipation of devolution (which was delayed) that my very good friend the late Bert Gemmell was promoted from Chief Passenger Manager at York to a post in Scotland. He had been instrumental in allowing the 'Talking of Trains' class to charter the GM Saloon in 1974 and subsequently. Initially this was a Wickham DMU. When he arrived in Scotland he provided us with two saloons and a loco and (in conjunction with sleepers from London) we left Perth in these for the first time on 21 April 1979 bound for Forfar, Newburgh, Alloa, Kilmarnock and Carlisle. I've included below a number of pictures of our Scottish specials in the 1980s, by which time dining and kitchen cars had been added so that we travelled in style to the Kyle, the Far North, Oban and Fort William, among other places.

Many people visiting Scotland on holiday pass from Carlisle to the Highlands without even noticing Galloway and its associated areas. I have therefore included seven views of the former Glasgow & South Western main line up the Nith Valley from Dumfries and that company's line to Stranraer. I call the latter the forgotten railway – freight traffic has ceased and most people now fly to Ireland or cross from Cairn Ryan. The lonely country it penetrates has changed little since the railway was built, and a drive through Glen Whilly, for instance, turns the clock back to quieter times.

By contrast the main line from Perth to Inverness thrives, trains originating in Glasgow via Stirling and others in Edinburgh via Ladybank over a line that was closed to regular passenger traffic for some years. There is freight, too, though the Safeway train has been withdrawn. Perhaps Eddie Stobart's service (see the Introduction) will be extended in due time. I have selected five pictures from the 1980s to illustrate this route.

It was anticipated that the upgrade of the A9, with bridges across the Beauly, Cromarty and Dornoch Firths – thus shortening the journey north of Inverness by many miles – would militate against the continuation of the train service, especially as the opportunity was lost to 'cut the corner' between Tain and Rogart by a joint road/rail bridge. But this does not seem to be the case. This is especially true of heavy freight, which I understand the police have banned from the A9, where lorries may jackknife on a sharp bend by the coast north of Helmsdale. Wick and Thurso, with their many industries, will not wish to be cut off from the rest of the UK! Ten pictures illustrate this route.

Ross, Borders; HST, 08.30 Aberdeen-King's Cross, 26 July 1983.
I have several friends in Berwick-on-Tweed, so often visit there, and on this occasion we went to see the landslip affecting the East Coast Main Line near Burnmouth. In order to get other photographs we took a footpath on to a nearby headland, and on our return were challenged by a workman as to what we were doing there, and were we locals? This aroused my curiosity, and when I showed the resultant pictures at the 'Talking of Trains' class I was advised by a safety officer that some dubious practices were visible! 8124

Above **Longniddry, Lothian; Class 26, down coal train, 25 July 1983.**
The character on the platform is Andrew Wylde who, I'm told, now drives a 'Deltic' from time to time. These local stations east of Edinburgh are served today by electric suburban trains bound to and from North Berwick (and occasionally Dunbar). *8201*

Below **Millerhill Yard, Lothian; Class 40 shunting, 25 July 1983.**
Thus are the mighty fallen! The yard is largely derelict and the tracks of the former 'Waverley' route to Carlisle neglected. Will they return to life with restoration to Galashiels? *8210*

Right Edinburgh Waverley, Lothian;
Class 40, JSG special Alnmouth-Stranraer,
12 May 1984.
The Class 40 is having to be replaced as a hose
caught fire while propelling from Drem to
North Berwick. We had travelled at such a
speed over breakfast from Alnmouth that we
caught up with the sleeper leaving the
Dunbar loop and had to wait there. I got the
impression that the crew wished to get home
early! *8237*

Below Edinburgh, Princes Street Gardens, Lothian; Class 40,
11.00 Edinburgh-Glasgow, and Class 47, train from Aberdeen,
1 October 1980.
There's a strange pattern of travel here. On Monday night I took the
car by Motorail sleeper from London to Newcastle and drove back to
York via Nawton with breakfast in Stokesley. Then I boarded the 13.15

train to Edinburgh, had lunch, and stayed in the city on business until
Friday, during which time I found the opportunity to take this picture.
The following Sunday I left the car in the BR compound in York and
took the sleeper from Leeds to London. I cannot trace how the car got
back home to Kingston... *10288*

Above Montrose, Tayside; Class 26 No 26038 and limestone wagons, 30 August 1989.
I'm here at the behest of the BR freight journal to record this working, which had just been inaugurated. I cannot now recall where it went southwards. *10562/11*

Below Montrose, Tayside; Class 47 No 47582 *County of Norfolk*, 11.10 Aberdeen-Glasgow (Queen Street), 30 August 1989.
While I had my track permit I thought I might as well photograph other workings in the station area, though the signalman rightly became excited at my presence as I discovered that the station staff had not notified him of my whereabouts. *10562/12*

Above Annan, Dumfries & Galloway; Class 47 No 47482,
11.55 Carlisle-Glasgow (Central), 23 September 1988.
I'm motoring between Farlam Hall and the Selkirk Arms,
Kirkcudbright, with Cyril Walmesley – we've gone to see trains on the
Stranraer line (see below). On the Sunday Cyril was due to get the
London train from Dumfries, as West Coast trains had been diverted.
In the event the diversions had been cancelled and to connect with the
express at Lockerbie I had to drive faster than I have ever done before
or since. We just made it! Sadly I never saw Cyril alive again (he was
in his 80s), and I can only hope that this event was not a contributory
factor. I became ill at Farlam Hall. 9747

Below Holywood, Dumfries & Galloway; Class 47,
14.58 Blackpool North-Glasgow (Central), 8 August 1981.
This is a holiday train taking its customers home. As far as I know this
signal box survives, and even the level crossing gates it controls. The
road goes nowhere in particular. At the time there was an up loop here.
Next day I left Carlisle at 14.59 on the Motorail to Kensington
(Olympia), arriving at 19.59, having been looped for other trains to
overtake at Colwich and Rugby. 9954

Above Drumshinnock, Dumfries & Galloway; Class 26,
15.34 Kilmarnock-Carlisle, 8 August 1981.
I wonder whether this train actually came from Stranraer via Ayr. As
you can surmise I am spending the day in Nithsdale and for the most
part it is good weather. This picture is taken at a lonely location not far
from Carron Bridge and Drumlanrig Tunnel. *9971*

Below Ha Cleuch Viaduct, Dumfries & Galloway; Class 47,
10.15 Euston-Stranraer Harbour, 8 August 1981.
The locomotive appears to be carrying some kind of snowplough,
though in August this would seem strange... No London trains now
run to the port, though Newcastle is still connected. One such train
calls at Brampton Junction in the early evening, and a loudspeaker
there conveys the words of a faraway voice recalling all the stops to
Stranraer. 9979

Right **Stranraer Harbour, Dumfries & Galloway; Class 27, JSG special from Alnmouth, 12 May 1984.**
We have reached here at last, little knowing that we would be held up for a long time at Falkland Junction on our final leg to Kilmarnock (for the London sleeper) by crew problems. We were then delayed again at Barassie Junction while something came towards us on the single line. I felt sorry for passengers in a local DMU behind us, which could not overtake. It was only due to the interests of our catering staff that the saloons were allowed to proceed at once to Glasgow, even though it meant that the London sleeper had to be held at Barrhead. The class had drinking time! Look at all the cars awaiting export to Northern Ireland. There are no longer any regular scheduled trains for this traffic. *9811*

Below **South Boreland, Dumfries & Galloway; Class 47, 10.55 Stranraer Harbour-Euston, 24 September 1988.**
We're not far from the junction at Dunragit with the direct line from Dumfries (closed entirely in 1965). When I chartered specials I made a point of following the proposed route by car. On the occasion of the train illustrated above I had failed to do so, therefore I relied on BR to tell me where platforms survived at which we could take a break. Dunragit was agreed (no platforms survived in the event) and Glen Whilly rejected (there were platforms there). Never mind, we had a wonderful time – and it would have interrupted dinner! *9820*

Left Glen Whilly, Dumfries & Galloway; Class 47 No 47518, 14.25 Stranraer-Glasgow (Central), 24 September 1988. This station was closed completely in 1965 but the loop is retained and, as far as I am aware, a signalman still mans the box. It is a very sparsely populated area, the station approach is unmetalled and a secondary entrance is via a ford. I love it! Do notice in the picture that tokens are about to be exchanged for the respective single lines. I would question whether illumination is by electricity. *9842*

Below Langbank, Strathclyde; Class 27, JSG special from Gourock to Dundee, 11 May 1985.
Because there were problems at the outset regarding the Scottish locos on our train at Alnmouth, we kept changing engines all day and the one left behind at the buffers at Gourock is at the signal behind us.

This proved to be our last charter, but we were unaware of this when we toasted the crew (dining-car and train) at North Queensferry. Typically I was not informed until the Glasgow outskirts were reached that we could not follow the agreed route through the suburbs because a signalman had not come on duty. *9945*

Right Glasgow (Queen Street),
Strathclyde; Class 27 No 27034,
JSG special to Glenfinnan/Oban,
25 April 1981.
This was our first charter to include a dining-
car and kitchen-car so that we could have
breakfast as soon as we boarded and complete
this by Bridge of Orchy. Because one of the
saloons had no corridor connection I had to
arrange station stops for everyone to transfer
to and from the diner at appropriate times! It
proved to be a magnificent day with sunshine
on the snowy tops of Rannoch Moor. To be
sipping coffee and looking out of the saloon
on to the mountainous landscape was
perfection. *11247*

Below Crianlarich, Central; Class 37, freight to Fort William,
and JSG special, 25 April 1981.
The crew of our train from Glenfinnan have transferred to the freight to get them home, while those who brought it here now take us to Oban. The famous refreshment room stands amidst the island platform. *11261*

Above Bridge of Orchy, Strathclyde; Class 37 No 37027, down freight, 17 May 1985.
This is a picture taken during my trip with Trevor to photograph the inaugural 'Royal Scotsman'. *11287*

Below Gorton loop, Strathclyde; Class 27 No 27034, JSG special from Glenfinnan to Oban, 25 April 1981.
At the risk of showing too many pictures of this special, I felt I had to include this one because of its rarity value. This isolated loop between Rannoch and Bridge of Orchy is little used and there are many stories about its past in the days of frequent snowdrifts and the like. We just had to stop there! *11294*

Above Tulloch, Highland; Class 37 Nos 37300 and 37291, up freight, 16 May 1985.
While the railway runs direct from Bridge of Orchy to Tulloch, we have had to drive right round via Fort William through Glen Coe. But it is worth it for this and the next picture. *11321*

Below Tulloch, Highland; Class 37 No 37191, westbound 'Royal Scotsman', 16 May 1985.
In the distance the line turns right to begin the ascent of Rannoch Moor. I suspect this photo is no longer possible if the trees in the foreground have matured and blocked the view. *11322*

Above Glenfinnan, Highland; Class 37, Mallaig-Fort William, 13 July 1984.
My diary simply reads, 'To see *Maude* at Glenfinnan; saw 10.05 to Mallaig by the chapel; tea & cake at Arisaig and walked on beach from where Bonnie Prince Charlie escaped; veal for dinner.' *11383*

Left Dunkeld, Tayside; Class 26, JSG special from Perth to Burghead, 26 April 1980.
This is our first special in Scotland in connection with sleepers from Euston. Staff at Perth advised me that the rear saloon – 1999 – was destined for the National Railway Museum, but I have never seen it there. It has a corridor connection at one end so that you can take sherry with the view, then transfer next door for dinner! *10826*

Above Dalnaspidal, Tayside; Class 47, 09.30 Inverness-Glasgow, 26 April 1980.
We've stopped here to photograph the passing express, which is running late! The station closed in 1965. Our class secretary, Audrey, transferred to the cab at this point, and soon afterwards loco problems occurred with water shortage, but were put right at Aviemore. *10859*

Below Carrbridge, Highland; Class 47, 10.35 Inverness-Euston 'Clansman', 26 April 1980.
We were looped here – do notice that to allow the express a straight run we are on the right. 'The Clansman' ran via Birmingham and last operated in May 1992 – its demise passed without notice. The London train now runs via the East Coast. *10886*

Above Moy Hall, Highland; Class 47 No 47148, 13.10 Glasgow (Queen Street)-Inverness, 1 September 1981.
I've been staying at the Invershin Hotel with Gavin, who left on the first train to Inverness and home. I then drove south and eventually joined the Motorail sleeper from Inverness at 20.20 to York. It was a super sunny afternoon, so this picture and the next one are bright. *10902*

Below Dalriach Crossing, Highland; Class 47, 15.05 Inverness-Glasgow (Queen Street), 1 September 1981.
The track to this crossing is so narrow and without passing places prior to the gates that I have had to back the car about 100 yards so as to face the right way if I had to leave quickly to make way for someone else. In the event no one came. *10904*

Above Burghead, Grampian; Class 27, JSG special to Dufftown,
26 April 1980.
We've decided to include more pictures than usual of my specials so as
to show unusual places. The branch here was kept for grain for whisky,
sent regularly to Doncaster. Passenger trains ceased as long ago as 1931.
When I crossed the junction near Alves by train in September 2006 I
noticed that a rail had been lifted from the branch. Our special was
propelled to Burghead while up and down trains crossed at Forres and
each passed the junction – good timing! *10796*

Below Drummuir, Grampian; Class 27, JSG special to Dufftown,
26 April 1980.
The station closed in 1968 but re-opened as the temporary terminus of
the preserved railway from Dufftown before it managed to reach Keith
itself. It's surrounded by woodland. *10753*

Above **Ardnagrask, Highland; Class 26, 11.08 Kyle of Lochalsh-Inverness, 29 August 1981.**
Gavin and I have come on the 23.55 Motorail sleeper from York to Inverness (arrive 09.15), and are now on our way to the Invershin Hotel. Golf-courses are a feature of Scotland, and to find the railway adjacent is not unusual. *10932*

Below **Muir of Ord, Highland; Class 37 No 37261, inaugural 'Royal Scotsman' to the Kyle, 19 May 1985.**
We have seen the train at Elgin and will do so again at Achanalt and Strathcarron, by which time the sun was fully out and lighting up the loch. Trains on the branch on a Sunday were quite a novelty at the time. *10933*

Tain, Highland; Class 26 No 26039, 11.45 ex-Wick/11.48 ex-Thurso to Inverness, 29 August 1981.
We're still on our way to Invershin! Do notice the semaphore signals, which have long been replaced by electronic token working. *11091*

Kyle of Lochalsh, Highland; Class 26 No 26038, JSG special to Perth, 23 April 1983.
The previous year, as you will witness below, we based the charter on Inverness and took the London sleeper from there. In consequence meals had to be taken early and rushed. So this time, although starting from Inverness, we are returning to Perth (and including a run on the newly opened Strathspey Railway to Boat of Garten). Half the 'Talking of Trains' group travelled from King's Cross (or York) to Edinburgh and the other from Euston to Glasgow so as not to overload the Inverness sleepers from those Scottish cities. The sleepers joined up in the night at Perth and we all met on the platform at Inverness! *11074*

Above Ardgay, Highland; Class 26, 05.30 ex-Wick/05.33
ex-Thurso to Inverness, 24 April 1982.

It's my 50th birthday and my special to the Far North is being passed
in a station that used to be known as Bonar Bridge, which I think was
better. When we were waiting to leave Inverness another special stood
on the adjacent track. The lady organiser of that took me to task,
saying that we had taken her path to the Far North so that she had to
go to Kyle of Lochalsh. I could only sympathise as I had no knowledge
of local politics. *11105*

Below Invercharron, Highland; Class 26, 05.30 ex-Wick/05.33
ex-Thurso to Inverness, 29 August 1980.

I am at the Invershin Hotel yet again and have come out before
breakfast with Cyril to photograph this working, with the waters of the
Kyle of Sutherland in the background. Later we were to go to Rogart
and Dornoch, where I bought a shirt and some ties! *11112*

Above Lairg, Highland; Class 26 Nos 26021 and 26037, 17.20 Inverness-Wick/Thurso, 31 August 1981.
It's the late Summer holiday (though not in Scotland), and the tablet exchange is about to take place. According to 'Freightmaster' there is now only one freight train north of Inverness each week and on a Monday. It leaves Mossend at 01.20 and returns from Lairg at 15.39, conveying empty four-wheel tanks. Hitherto Safeway had run north of here, but the acquisition by Morrison's put a stop to that. *11129*

Below Dalmore, Highland; Class 26s, 11.15 ex-Wick/11.18 ex-Thurso to Inverness, 30 August 1981.
It is a glorious Sunday morning and we are looking down and along Strath Fleet, which passes through a loch and enters the Dornoch Firth. Do notice the buffet car. If you consult old timetables you will find incredible detail as to when the attendant opened up – sometimes at Kildonan, at others at Kinbrace, depending on the date. I wonder whether he ever knew of this bureaucracy or just served from Georgemas? *11143*

Glen Loth bridge, Highland; Class 26, 11.45 ex-Wick/11.48 ex-Thurso to Inverness, 30 August 1980.
I have trespassed and had to steel myself to cross the bridge to reach this location. It has no parapets and I do not relish uninhibited heights.

It was worth it, though, and I retraced my steps the moment the train had passed. The waters of Glen Loth are about to empty into the North Sea. *11172*

Above Portgower, Highland; Class 26, 11.45 ex-Wick/11.48 ex-Thurso to Inverness, 31 August 1981.
We often hear of the Great Western by the sea at Dawlish, but rarely of the line climbing from Helmsdale through Lothbeg to Brora and beyond – the scenery is probably better. Perhaps it's too cold to bathe. *11176*

Below Kinbrace, Highland; Class 26, 11.10 Inverness-Wick/Thurso, 31 August 1981.
The railway turns inland at Helmsdale to follow the Strath of Kildonan, then the Bannock Burn to Forsinard. Notice how the line wanders to take advantage of firm ground amongst the boggy surroundings. We shall leave the railway here to complete the road circuit via Altnaharra back to Lairg (for the evening train above) and Invershin. *11187*

Above Altnabreac, Highland; Class 26 No 26041, JSG special to Wick, 24 April 1982.

Trains call here only by request, and beware those who alight without certainty of journey or adequate shelter. It really is bleak, and there is only one dwelling in view. I doubt whether passengers have been summoned to lunch at this place, but this was the case on my birthday. *11209*

Below Thurso, Highland; Class 26 No 26041, JSG special, and Class 26, afternoon train to Inverness, 24 April 1982.

David Short concentrates on photography while others wander round. The Station Master took me aside to stress the importance of time-keeping so that we crossed the next northbound train at Forsinard without delay. This we did and had our class photo afterwards. *11235*

INDEX

Roman numerals indicate the colour pages.